WITHDRAWN
BOOK
£1

THE SCHWARTZ
STOCK MARKET HANDBOOK

THE SCHWARTZ STOCK MARKET HANDBOOK

1995 Edition

by
David Schwartz

Burleigh Publishing Company

© Burleigh Publishing Company 1994

Compiled and edited by David Schwartz
Published by Burleigh Publishing Company,
Burleigh Hall, Burleigh, Stroud, Gloucestershire GL5 2PF

ISBN 0 9523961 0 6

A CIP record for this book is available from the British Library

Produced by Trigon Press, Beckenham, Kent
Printed in England

Notice

Whilst every effort has been made to ensure that information in this book
is correct, no liability can be accepted for any loss incurred in any way
whatsoever by any person relying solely on the information contained herein.

CONTENTS

INTRODUCTION

Our first book in this series, the *1994 Investor's Diary*, was designed as a combination week-at-a-glance appointment diary, record-keeping journal, and book about stock market trends.

Follow-up research was quite revealing. Readers loved the historical stock market trends. 'Lots more' was the typical request. Regarding our week-at-a-glance diary and back-of-the-book record-keeping schedules, compliments were harder to find. The typical response was: 'No interest in the diary. Forced to take it for access to stock market data.'

A British visitor to the American Wild West, around the turn of the century, reportedly asked a local cowboy how he managed to train his mule to be so obedient. Mules, or jackass's, as the locals like to call them, can be the most wilful and cantankerous of all animals, but not this one.

'It's easy,' said the cowboy. 'The secret is to catch his attention.'

'How do you do that?' asked the visitor.

'Speak softly so that he has to listen carefully,' answered the cowboy, 'and then whack him on the head a couple of times with a two-by-four.'

Our research and the cowboy's two-by-four have one important point in common. Your comments captured our attention and led us down a slightly different road from the one we originally planned to travel.

The 1995 edition has a new name and format, expanded coverage of historical stock market trends and lots of charts to simplify the communication of complicated information. We hope it pleases you.

About our data sources: It is not easy to analyse stock market trends accurately, over the long-term. The various share price indices available to investors are forever being changed, improved or in some cases, terminated in response to declining investor interest. The 'old standards' are neither very old nor very standardised. We find no single index that has been available for the full 75-year period studied in this handbook.

We made the best of a difficult situation by piecing together a 75-year-long monthly price trend index from three sources: from 1919 to 1924, an index compiled by *British Banker Magazine*. From 1925 to March, 1962, the *Investors Chronicle Industrial Index* which was periodically changed and up-dated. From April, 1962 to the present, the *FT- Non-Financial Index* (formerly the FT-'500') which also was periodically up-dated. The *British Banker* and *Investors Chronicle* series' are both long out of print. They were located by researchers at Barclays de Zoete Wedd Securities Limited. We are grateful to them, especially to Michael Hughes, Managing Director – Economics and Strategy for making this data available to Stock Market Handbook readers.

We prefer the *FT-Non-Financial Index* to the slightly broader *FT-SE A All Shares Index* for forecasting purposes. You can usually find it on the back page of the *Financial Times*.

All short-term (daily or partial month) price trends discussed in this book are derived from the *FT Ordinary Share Index* which has been running since July 1st, 1935. We agree that there are deficiencies associated with this index, not the least of which is that it is based on only 30 leading companies. Still, it is the only continuous daily index that has been published for this length of time. The *FT-SE 100*, in contrast, has been in existence for a little over one decade.

One closing thought. We did our best but, alas, we aren't perfect. We probably overlooked some important trends, misinterpreted some of those we did report on, and omitted to report critical information that you were desperate to have.

Please write or telephone if you have any requests or suggestions. Criticisms are especially welcome but, please, no two-by-fours to catch our attention! Your comments will help us to make next year's edition even better.

David Schwartz, Editor
September, 1994

FREE QUARTERLY NEWSLETTER

Readers of *The Schwartz Stock Market Handbook* are invited to request a free quarterly newsletter that we publish towards the end of each quarter of the year – March, June, September, and December.

Each edition will discuss one or two trends of topical interest to stock market investors, trends which are not covered in this book.

In case you are wondering, 'What's the catch?', the answer is simple. Our goal is to build an on-going relationship with our readers and we believe that providing this FREE service will help us to achieve our long-term objectives.

To obtain your copies, please mail us a separate stamped, pre-addressed A4-sized envelope for each issue to:

Quarterly Newsletter
Schwartz Stock Market Handbook
Burleigh Publishing Company
Burleigh Hall
Stroud
Gloucestershire GL5 2PF

DISCLAIMER

This book is essentially a review of past stock market trends. It is based upon an historical analysis of every closing price on the various share price indices available at the time this book was prepared.

Every statement we make about possible future price movements is a statistical projection derived from past trends. No one knows if any of these relationships will continue in the future. Our observations are not intended to be recommendations to buy or sell any particular stock or the market as a whole.

Statements about profits or losses associated with any buy or sell action are calculated before all fees and taxes of any kind.

Remember that the price of any stock market investment can go down as well as up. You can easily lose some or all of your investment. This is especially true of Call and Put options which are very volatile.

Be sure to discuss the risk of any investment you are considering with a qualified adviser before making any investment decision.

CHAPTER ONE – HISTORIC TRENDS IMPROVE FUTURE PROFITS

According to conventional wisdom, life provides few guarantees aside from death and taxes. Most investors are quick to agree.

Conventional wisdom is wrong.

If you follow stock market trends over the long-term, you will find vast quantities of evidence to contradict this broadly-held belief. You might have to jiggle the data a bit or look at it from a different perspective but the effort is well worth the trouble. There are many repetitive trends that occur on a regular basis. Some appear like clock-work at the same time of month, year or point in the economic cycle. Others, perhaps not as precise or punctual as a fine Swiss clock, pop up a lot more often than one could expect if they were occurring on a purely random basis.

Take the month of January for example. If share prices randomly fluctuate around a basic long-term trend, as many market theorists claim, January would be as profitable as the other 11 months of the year. Its profits might be higher than average in some years and worse than average in other years. But over the very long-run, say half-a-century or more, one would expect January's prices to rise or fall to the same degree as they do in the other 11 months.

So much for theory. The reality of the stock market is different – a lot different. January is not like other months. Investors usually make money in January. Between 1919 and 1993, January prices rose 72% of the time. Historically, January has been the best month of the year in which to invest in shares. By way of contrast, prices rise just 52% of the time in June. A hypothetical £1,000 investment back in 1919, with the money invested in shares each January, and taken out of the market the other 11 months, would have grown to £5,376 by 1993. A comparable June investment would have shrunk to £552 (see Figure 1.1).

No one knows for certain why January is so good to investors. Perhaps pension fund cash in-flows are extra heavy at the turn of the year. Or maybe the profusion of fresh company

January is not like other months

1

Figure 1.1

PROFITABILITY VARIES BY MONTH
1993 value of £1,000 monthly investment in 1919

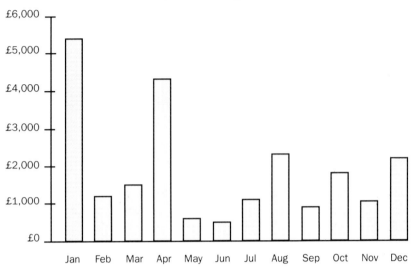

Figure 1.1: January is the year's most profitable month. A hypothetical January investment, starting with £1,000 in 1919 would
have grown to £5,376 by 1993. Number Two-ranked April also has
been very profitable but its trend is likely to change for the worse
now that Budget Day has been shifted to November (*see Chapter
5*). August and December round out the Big Four. May, June, and
September are money-losers in the long-run.

results and forecasts give investors a clearer vision of the future,
making them more willing to commit fresh funds to shares. It
may sound persuasive but, if it is true, why is December, with
fewer results/forecasts also so good to investors? And what
makes August investments so profitable and September investments so poor? No one really knows, although all of these
trends have been operative for many years.

More profits early
in decade

Another trend that is difficult to explain is the tendency for
share prices to be strongest in the beginning of each decade.
Between 1920 to 1989, prices either rose very weakly (by no
more than 5%) or fell in 32 years. Relatively few of these poor
years ended with a one to five, eg, 1921 to 1925. Why is the
beginning of each decade better for share prices than the end?
No one knows (*see Figure 1.2*).

The 1990s are true to form, so far. Prices fell in 1990 and rose in 1991 to 1993. Are 1994 and '95 immune to poor results? Certainly not. In fact, as we go to press, 1994 is looking rather disappointing. But over the long-run, the odds seem to favour better results near the beginning of a decade. 1995, incidentally, is a member of a very exclusive club – years ending with a five have never experienced a price fall. Wall Street has a similar love for years ending in a five. Between 1885 and 1985, the Wall Street record is 11 up and no downs.

Could this trend be a statistical fluke because of an insufficient number of observations? Perhaps. We will be able to mathematically prove our case in another century or so, as the number of observations increases, assuming it is a trend and it remains intact. For the moment, you have all the data that exists. Decide for yourself.

Some trends are easier to explain, like the fact that the UK stock market rises every year before a Leap Year. It's a phenomenon that has been going on since 1951. At the approach of every Leap Year, share prices celebrate by rising.

Figure 1.2   **PRICE SHIFTS BY YEAR IN DECADE: 1920–1989**

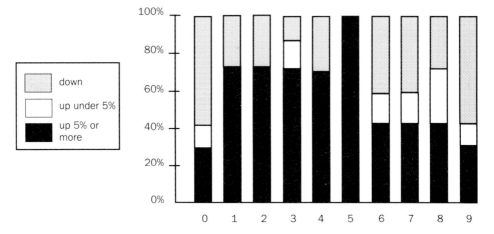

Figure 1.2: In the last 70 years, share prices rose most often in the second to sixth year of a decade. No one knows why. The two worst years of the decade are the first and the last. Investors have never lost money in years ending in five, eg 1965, 1975, 1985.

Figure 1.3 **AVERAGE ANNUAL UK PRICE RISE AND THE US PRESIDENTIAL CYCLE**

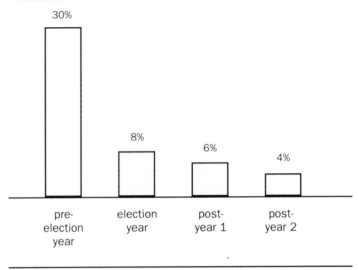

The source of this gift to investors is not extra-terrestrial or astrological. It's a good deal closer, Washington DC to be precise. For readers who would like to thank their benefactor, write to him at 1600 Pennsylvania Avenue, also known as the White House.

To understand why American Presidents are so nice to British investors, you must first understand the American electoral process. Unlike our system, the US presidential term of office is fixed by law. Elections take place every four years in Leap Year. Everyone in government knows the exact date of the next election as soon as they enter office, and can take whatever steps are necessary to create the best economic situation possible when voters next step up to the ballot box.

Election time   It's questionable whether any government can control the economy over the long run. A potent combination of inadequate economic theory, insufficient information about the current state of the economy, and lack of political will to do the unpopular constantly undermines the best of intentions. But in the short -term, governments have learned how to take steps to accelerate an economy, regardless of the long-term effects. And if a government knows it is facing a re-election campaign, it isn't very difficult to forecast whether or not it will use this ability to manipulate the economy.

Stock market anticipates

Since the stock market anticipates changes in the real economy by up to a year, it's usually a good time to own shares in the year before a presidential election (*see Figure 1.3*). Are you wondering why UK investors benefit from a US domestic issue? There are two main reasons: the large influence of the American economy on the profits of UK-owned multi-nationals (roughly 16% of all UK profits emanate from the US, 25% among the larger FT-SE 100 companies), and the weight of outward investment money from the US in good economic years.

Although the focus of this book is on the UK stock market, we can't resist a brief digression. For readers inclined to make a small wager on the winner of the 1996 US Presidential race, here is a useful forecasting tool.

Dismal prospects for the incumbent

Since 1951, share prices rose every fourth year, 11 times in a row. The three worst years for UK investors were 1951, 1979 and 1987 (*see Figure 1.4*). The common element linking each of these poor years was the dismal prospects in America for the party in power. History shows that Democrat Harry Truman chose not to run for re-election in 1952, knowing he would lose to the Republican challenger Dwight Eisenhower. Adalai Stevenson ran in his place, and lost decisively.

In 1980, President Jimmy Carter lost his re-election bid against Ronald Reagan.

In 1988, Ronald Reagan's vice-president, George Bush ran against the Democrat, Michael Dukakas. Although Bush won, commentators widely reported at the time that Dukakas ran an inept campaign. As one analyst put it, Dukakas succeeded in pulling defeat from the jaws of victory. If 1995 provides a poor return to UK investors, history suggests Bill Clinton might be a one-term president.

As far as the UK stock market is concerned, repetitive trends are not just limited to monthly or yearly cycles. They exist on a daily and weekly basis too.

Daily trends

If daily share price fluctuations are strictly random, there would be no difference in profitability by day of week. Over the long-run, investors would make or lose money on Monday as often as on Tuesday or Wednesday. But there are big inter-day differences in profitability, and they have been occurring for over half a century. Between 1935 – 93, the best trading days of

Figure 1.4　　　**UK STOCK MARKET PERFORMANCE IN YEAR BEFORE US PRESIDENTIAL ELECTION**

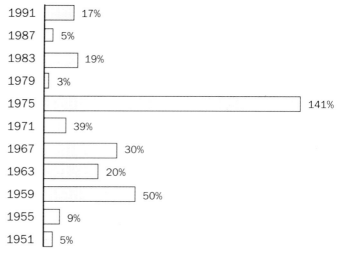

Figure 1.4: Since World War II, the three worst pre-election years for UK investors were 1951, 1979, and 1987. In each case, the American political party in power had considerable difficulty in the following year's election. The incumbent was thrown out of office in 1951 and 1979. Ronald Reagan's chosen successor, George Bush, squeezed out a 1987 victory, helped with a poor effort by an inept opponent.

---

the week have been on Wednesday and Friday. Prices rise 53% of the time each day. In contrast, Monday's prices rise just 44% of the time, the week's worst performance (*see Figure 1.5*). Don't be too quick to conclude that 53% is not very different from 44%. Another way to look at it this data is that Wednesday's performance is 20% better than Monday's.

The difference in profitability is not unique to our stock market. Wall Street also exhibits wide fluctuations on a day-of-week basis.

Weekly trends　　　The best week of the year for British investors is the last week of December. Prices rise 81% of the time. This trend has been building since 1935 when daily indices were first introduced to the UK. In contrast, the worst week of the year is the third week of May when prices rise just 40% of the time. While you might profit in some years, a May investment is a money-losing proposition in the long-run. Imagine opening a £1,000 trading

Figure 1.5 **PERCENTAGE OF TIME PRICES RISE EACH TRADING DAY**

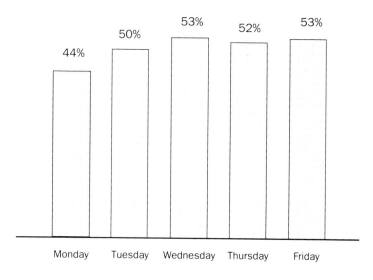

Figure 1.5: Monday is the week's worst day. If you are thinking of selling shares, the odds favour doing so before the weekend. On the other hand, if you are thinking about buying shares late Friday afternoon, there is a good chance of purchasing those shares at a lower price by waiting until Monday.

account in 1935, shifting the entire contents into shares each year during the last week of December, and withdrawing for the rest of the year. It's an academic exercise of course, but it reveals an interesting point. By 1993, your investment would have grown to £1,835, quite high considering that your capital was at risk for just 230 trading days. The same investment, made in the third week of May, would have shrunk to just £683.

'4 in 10' rule   As you can see, there are many clues hidden in the financial section of your daily newspaper. The purpose of this book is to reveal some of them to you. Before moving on, here is one provocative annual trend that we hope you take a long look at, the tendency for share prices to fall about four years out of every 10 (*see Figure 1.6*). It is a steady trend that has been operative since the 1920s. There was a single deviation from the norm in the 1980s. Some investors, especially those born after World War II, have come to believe share ownership is a one-way bet, and that stock market declines, no matter how sharp, are short-

Figure 1.6   **STOCK MARKETS FALL AS WELL AS RISE**
The 1980s were an exception

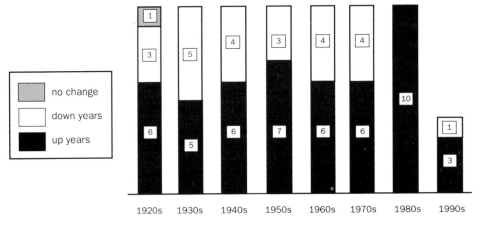

Figure 1.6: The 1980s were the first decade since records began with no down years. Are the '80s the pattern of the future or will we return to the patterns of the past? No one knows for sure. If you believe the pattern of the past will prevail, the data suggests that prices will fall in four out of 10 years in each decade.

term setbacks. If you believe share prices will always rise, you must believe one or more of the following:

▶ The UK political environment has changed – permanently. Our leaders are less politically motivated. They will no longer take action which hurts our economy in the long-run, for short-term political advantage. They will have the political courage to take unpopular action.

▶ Government officials have more technical skill in managing and lengthening the economic cycle than in the past. We no longer live in a stop/start economy.

▶ Investors have changed. They are more sanguine about the future and are willing to pump fresh money into shares during all phases of the economic cycle, even if the cycle is five or more years old.

▶ The world economy has changed. It will always steadily grow. Our export markets will continue to grow.

▶ International investors, who account for a large and growing share of all purchases of UK shares, will keep pumping money into the UK market.

The fact of the matter is that prices fall in some years. The 1980s were probably a one-in-a-lifetime event. How far will they fall in the next Bear Market? No one knows. Figure 1.7 provides one perspective by plotting the month-by-month performance of the UK stock market from 1919 to 1993 without any adjustment for inflation. As you can see, there have been enormous increases since the end of 1974. About 95% of the total rise in share prices over the last three-quarters of the century has occurred in this period.

Beware – the stock market can fall

We have no wish to be alarmist and are not forecasting a major stock market collapse, but it is important that investors see how steep a decline is possible if share prices ever dropped to their very long-term historic trend line. Some readers may be thinking it can never happen. The reasons are quick to flow – depression, riots in the streets, the end of capitalism. But look again at the chart, especially the big decline of 1973–74. Notice how prices fell to the area of the long-term trend. In other words, not only can it happen, it *did* happen. So don't be too quick to conclude that a really big fall can't happen. A better way to express the concept is to say the odds are *against* it happening. But it *could* happen.

We show the last two charts to establish that stock markets can be dangerous. Big profits can be made but so can big losses.

Having captured your attention with the verbal equivalent of the two-by-four discussed in our Introduction, we turn to the main point of this book, the opportunities and pitfalls associated with stock market investing during 1995. You need not fret. Many profit enhancing trends will be available in 1995. As you read and study them, keep in mind the three guiding principles that underly every historical price trend analysis.

No guarantees

▶ No one can flawlessly forecast where share prices are heading. Historically-based probabilities define the odds of an up or down move based on past performance trends. They increase the likelihood that investors make the right choice but do not guarantee success.

Trend-breaking news

▶ Although historical price trends provide strong clues about the direction of future share price moves, fresh economic or political news makes hash of these probabilities. Witness the market's reaction to our withdrawal from the ERM or to rumours of interest rate changes.

Success breeds failure

▶ Knowledge of a probable event often causes investor behaviour to change (perhaps buying shares in advance to catch an expected up-move). The effect of these behaviour changes is to alter the underlying pattern that created the trend in the first place. Historical analysis is a never ending process. Investors must keep studying the market to keep abreast of changing patterns.

Figure 1.7 **UK STOCK MARKET PRICE TREND: 1919–1993**

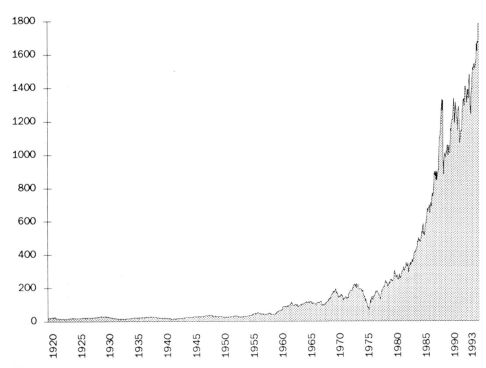

Chapter Two – January 1995

> In addition to being the best month of the year, January with December makes the best two-month stretch of the year. The second half of January has been the bigger profit-maker in recent years. There are a number of historic trends that signal an above-average likelihood of making a January profit.

Money-making time

January is usually money-making time, the year's most profitable month. Between 1919 and 1993, January prices rose 72% of the time. The average price rise was +2.47%, equal to 82 points on an FT-SE 100 in the area of 3300.

Some of January's superior performance is due to a dramatic +51.45% increase in 1975 which marked the end of the 1973–74 Bear Market. It was the biggest-ever one-month increase in share prices. But even if this extraordinary year is eliminated from the computation, the January record would still be a quite credible +1.81% average increase per year over the long-run.

The only money-losing decade for the January investor was back in the 1930s. Since then, the month has been consistently profitable. The constant January investor may not have profited every year, but did so on a decade-by-decade basis during the 1940s, '50s, '60s, '70s and '80s (*see Table 2.1*).

Recent record is getting better

As noted earlier, no one knows why share prices rise so often in January. Some analysts guess that the large number of end-of-year company results and forecasts for the year ahead give investors more confidence to commit new funds. Others point to increased pension fund cash in-flows. Whatever the cause, January's performance has been getting better in recent decades. In the 1960s, it was the number three-ranked month. In the 1970s, it moved up to number two. In the 1980s, it became the number one-ranked month, rising in nine out of 10 years, with an average monthly price rise of +5.52%.

The jury is still out for the 1990s. The record through 1993 is one up and three down, one of the worst four-year stretches in January's history. Is January losing its magic? Our opinion is that the long-term trend has not changed. The last very poor stretch of this magnitude was back in the 1930s when January's

Table 2.1   **JANUARY PRICE RISES AND DECLINES: 1919–1993**

	Average January price change	Up	Down
1920–29	2.19%	8	2
1930–39	-0.29%	5	5
1940–49	1.85%	10	–
1950–59	0.91%	6	4
1960–69	2.17%	8	2
1970–79	5.55%	7	3
1980–89	5.52%	9	1
1990–93	-0.19%	1	3
Average January price change	2.47%	54	21

Table 2.1: January investors last lost money during the 1930s. Since then, the month has been quite profitable. Investors did not profit every single year, but made money in every decade from the 1940s to 1980s. Even without 1975's extraordinary rise of 51.45%, January is a strong performer. The average price rise in the rest of the 1970s was 0.45%. Over the remaining 74 years, the average was 1.81%.

---

prices fell three years in a row. The pattern in those years was exemplified by continued weakness throughout the whole month. In contrast, the recent bout of weakness seems to occur early in the month – often a temporary setback after a strong December price rise. Are we right or wrong with our forecast? Only time will tell.

The one fly in the ointment is the shift to a late autumn Unified Budget. We don't know the effect of this switch on the January price trend, although history tells us stock market prices often rise in the weeks following Budget Day (see Chapter Twelve for specific Budget Day trends). Our suspicion is the month will remain a good profit-maker for investors but, here again, only time will tell for sure.

First-half weakness

In the short-run, pay careful attention to the first two quarters of the month where much of the recent weakness has clustered. The third and fourth quarters of the month continue to be profitable most of the time – especially the fourth quarter. In the last 20 years, fourth-quarter share prices fell just three

88% chance of
profit

times. The strong performance continued during the 1990s.

Believe it or not, it is possible to do even better than average with a January investment. One of the most accurate predictors of rising prices in January is a steadily rising price trend throughout the previous year. Look for *(a)* rising prices during the past month (December), past two months, past three months, past six months and past 12 months, and *(b)* prices up by at least 2% in the last two months and three months. If the necessary conditions are met, there is an 88% likelihood that January prices will rise.[1]

These conditions may seem onerous but, since 1920, have occurred 17 times. January prices rose in 15 of those years (88%). The average January share price increase in the 17 years with a strong prior year up-trend was +3.05%.

Rose (15)

Fell (2)

January's record after steadily rising prices in the past 12 months (since 1920)

The two exceptions are instructive and provide further support for the rule. In 1959, January prices fell by a tiny -0.1%. In 1993, poor trading conditions at the beginning of the month were reversed with a late month rally that moved prices into positive territory on February 1st – one day late!

---

[1] Reminder: All monthly calculations are based on the FT-Non-Financial Index, formerly the FT-'500'. Unless otherwise stated, they are based on data from 1919–1993. All daily, quarterly and bi-monthly calculations are based on the Ordinary Share Index, also known as the FT-30. Unless otherwise stated, they are based on data from 1936-1993. Both indices are usually found on the back page of the *Financial Times*. If you do not have price trends for the last 12 months readily available, we will provide them at no cost. Send a self-addressed, postage-paid envelope to:
    Closing Price Offer
    Burleigh Publishing Company
    Burleigh Hall
    Burleigh
    Stroud
    Gloucestershire GL5 2PF

Another trend to watch is the direction of prices during the preceding six months. If they rise moderately, by no more than 7%, the odds of a January price increase improve considerably. Here's the evidence. Since 1920, share prices rose by less than 7% in the six-month run-up to January on 19 occasions. January prices rose in 17 of those years (89%). The average annual price increase was +1.68%.

Rose (17)

Fell (2)

January's record after steadily rising prices in the past six months (since 1920)

What about the remaining years in which the 12-Month Rule and the 6-Month Rule did not apply? Since 1920, there were 46 such years. January share prices rose 30 times and fell 16 times. The average annual price increase was +2.65% but a large part of this increase was due to 1975's dramatic rise of +51.45%. If we eliminate this once-in-a-lifetime rally, the average increase for all other Januarys is +1.54%. In other words, even in years with weaker prospects, you would still make money in the long-run, but less of it, and on a more erratic basis.

Wide differences in profit

Although January is a good month in which to invest, there are wide differences in profit potential associated with in-vestments made during different segments of the month. To prove the point, January was divided into four quarters: January 1–8, 9–15, 16–23, and 24–31, and the price changes per quarter were analysed all the way back to 1936 (*see Table 2.2*).

Over the long-term, the first and last quarters of the month have been January's two most profitable segments. Both have been consistent money-makers. Investing in the two middle quarters produced less profit. But in the more recent past, third-quarter share price trends have been getting stronger.

Given the differences in profit potential between each quarter, and the recent trend changes, each segment will be examined separately.

Table 2.2

PERCENTAGE PRICE CHANGE: JANUARY 1936–1993

	January 1–8	January 9–15	January 16–23	January 24–31
Average annual price change				
1936–39	0.15%	-0.29%	-0.76%	0.34%
1940–49	0.52%	0.49%	-0.39%	-0.01%
1950–59	0.20%	-0.25%	-0.22%	0.08%
1960–69	0.59%	-0.08%	0.27%	0.97%
1970–79	0.69%	1.39%	0.77%	1.96%
1980–89	1.76%	0.83%	2.09%	1.83%
1990–93	0.35%	-0.59%	-0.16%	2.09%
Average quarterly price change	0.63%	0.35%	0.37%	1.00%
Number of years in which prices:				
rose	37	32	32	38
fell	21	26	26	20

Table 2.2: Over the long-term, the first and last quarters of the month have been the two most profitable segments. But in recent years, the third quarter's performance has improved.

FIRST QUARTER OF JANUARY – JANUARY 2ND TO 8TH

Prices have risen in 64% of all first quarters. A steady first-quarter investor made a profit in every single decade. Since records began, this part of the month has generated an average profit of +0.63% per year, equal to 21 points on an FT-SE 100 in the area of 3300.[2]

Some traders have also observed that share prices usually rise on the first trading day of the year, regardless of whether the day falls on January 2, 3 or 4. Are their perceptions accurate?

---

[2] Reminder: All daily, quarterly and bi-monthly price trends are based on the FT Ordinary Share index (FT-30) from 1936 to 1993 unless otherwise indicated.

Very much so. In the 59 years between 1936 and 1994, share prices fell just 17 times (29%) on the first trading day of the New Year.

Start the year with a profit

Although the odds are good that you will profit by holding shares on the year's first trading day, you can load the dice in your favour to an even greater degree by monitoring the price trend on the final two trading days before Christmas. History shows that if share prices decline during this two-day stretch, they will probably also fall on the first trading day of the New Year, after investors forget the holiday spirit and settle down to some serious trading.

There have been 16 declines on the two pre-Christmas trading days since 1935. On 10 of those occasions, the first trading day of the New Year also fell (63%). In the remaining 43 years prices fell just seven times (16%) on the first trading day after New Years Day.

Small chance of loss if prices rise on two pre-Christmas days

Pre-Xmas rise (16%)

Pre-Xmas fall (63%)

Likelihood of price drop on first trading day of new year if prices rose or fell on two pre-Christmas days

Does the length of the New Year's holiday trading break have any effect on the market's likelihood of rising or falling? Not at all. The market rises the same percentage of the time, regardless of the length of the holiday.

It's not just the first trading day of the month that tends to be profitable. Analysis of daily share price trends over the long-run, shows that each day in the quarter is profitable at least half the time. In fact, the fourth is the most profitable trading day of the entire month on an historical basis (*see Figure 2.1*).

Good long-term trend

Although the long-term trend is good, don't get too complacent. The 1990s have started off poorly for first-quarter investors. Prices fell three years in a row, something that has happened just twice before. Prices rose the following year each time and the trend continued on course so we are not very concerned that three falls in a row is signalling a trend change.

Furthermore, in the current bout of weakness, prices re-

Figure 2.1

PERCENTAGE OF TIME PRICES RISE EACH TRADING DAY IN JANUARY'S FIRST QUARTER

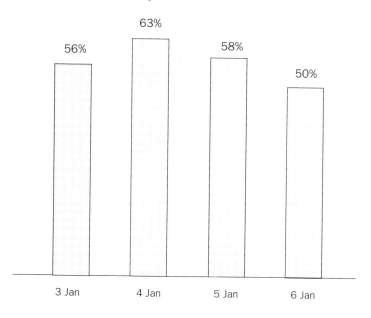

Figure 2.1: The likelihood of rising prices is high throughout the first quarter. January 4 is the most profitable day of the entire month. (Market closed in 1995 on missing dates.)

bounded soon after the quarter ended suggesting investors used the beginning of the new year for short-term profit-taking after a strong December up-move. For these reasons, we are not yet forecasting a trend change. We shall continue to watch the situation carefully.

Maximise your trading profits

For the present, here are some useful statistically-based rules of thumb to help you to maximise your trading profits in this quarter of the month. While they will not work every year, they will improve your track record over the long-run.

The size of the price shift in the second half of December does a good job of forecasting where first-quarter prices are heading. There have been 12 years when prices shifted moderately in the second half of December, by no more than -0.42% on the downside and no more than +0.92% on the up-side. Prices rose in the first quarter of January in 11 of those years.

Rose (11)

Fell (1)

First-quarter record after a price shift of -0.42% to +0.92% in
December's second half

Similarly, if prices rise by a tiny amount in the fourth quarter of
December, no more than +0.35%, a first-quarter increase
usually follows.

Rose (10)

Fell (1)

First-quarter record after a price rise of up to +0.35% in
December's fourth quarter

SECOND QUARTER OF JANUARY – JANUARY 9TH TO 15TH

The second quarter has the questionable distinction of being
January's worst-performing quarter. Although it is weak in a
relative sense, share prices do rise more often than they fall
(55% of the time between 1936 and 1993) and produce an
average annual profit of +0.35% per year.

At first glance, the performance of the second and third
quarters looks to be quite similar. But the third-quarter profit
trend has been improving and has become quite good to
investors in recent years (*see Table 2.3*). In contrast, the second-
quarter trend remains unchanged. In the last 20 years, its record
was nine up and 11 down. In the last 10 years, second-quarter
prices rose just five times.

No meaningful
trend change

During the Bull Market 1980s, January's second quarter
produced a reasonably sized average annual profit (+0.83% per
year), causing some analysts to wonder if the basic underlying
trend had improved. But be cautious in acting on this data. For
one thing, in a decade that saw a consistent pattern of profitability for the entire month, during the greatest Bull Market of the

Table 2.3

PERCENTAGE PRICE CHANGE FOR JANUARY SINCE 1980

	January 1–8	January 9–15	January 16–23	January 24–31
1980	0.34%	6.28%	2.06%	0.55%
1981	-3.20%	-2.35%	1.61%	2.33%
1982	0.19%	0.04%	6.70%	2.22%
1983	4.07%	-1.10%	0.85%	0.53%
1984	2.40%	1.74%	0.84%	2.02%
1985	1.98%	-0.97%	4.36%	-1.75%
1986	-0.67%	-1.26%	0.97%	3.62%
1987	6.93%	2.51%	1.35%	1.06%
1988	3.80%	0.79%	-1.09%	1.03%
1989	1.79%	2.59%	3.28%	6.68%
1990	1.48%	-2.47%	-3.02%	1.33%
1991	-2.20%	-1.01%	0.57%	4.19%
1992	-0.30%	2.90%	1.18%	1.69%
1993	-0.38%	-1.75%	0.64%	1.17%
Average quarterly price change				
1980–89	1.76%	0.83%	2.09%	1.83%
1980–93	1.16%	0.42%	1.45%	1.91%
Number of years in which prices:				
rose	9	7	12	13
fell	5	7	2	1

Table 2.3: The third-quarter profit trend has recently improved. The second half of January is now the major source of profits.

century, the second quarter fell four times – in 1981, 1983, 1985 and 1986. It was ranked third or fourth in profitability for eight of the decade's 10 years. In addition, the +0.83% average annual profit was the weakest (by far) of the month's four quarters. Since the 1987 crash, the record is three up and three down.

Despite this quarter's relatively weak performance, if you currently hold shares and are a long-term investor, in most years it would pay you to hold on to your position – given the good odds of a third- and fourth-quarter profit. But if you are contemplating making a purchase, you have, roughly, a 50:50 chance of profiting during this period. Fortunately, you can improve these odds by watching the direction of prices during January's first quarter. Every single time prices shifted by a small amount, second-quarter prices rose.

Watch the first quarter

Rose (15)

Fell (0) |

Second-quarter record after a price shift of -0.04% to +0.97% in the first quarter

In timing your decision to buy or sell shares during this point of the month, note that most of the losses occur in the middle of the quarter. Prices are most likely to rise at the very beginning and end of the quarter. So if you are thinking of buying around mid-month, don't be afraid to push things ahead by a day or two (*see Figure 2.2*).

Figure 2.2

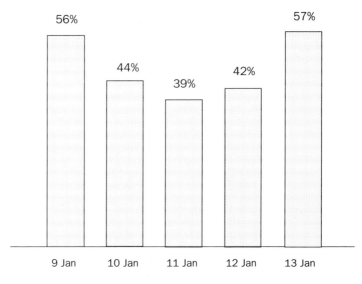

PERCENTAGE OF TIME PRICES RISE EACH TRADING DAY

Figure 2.2: Prices tend to fall most often during the middle of the second quarter.

THIRD QUARTER OF JANUARY – JANUARY 16TH TO 23RD

Over the long-term, the third-quarter record is not particularly impressive. It is ranked 21st-best quarter of the year (out of 48).

The source of the weakness is the last few days of the quarter. Prices have risen on 46% of all January 20ths and just 39% of all January 23rds *(see Figure 2.3)*. The problem spills over to the beginning of the fourth quarter of the month. When January 24th's sorry record is added (up 42% of the time), investors are exposed to the worst three trading days of the entire month by holding shares during this stretch.

Prior to the 1980s, a decade-by-decade analysis of third-quarter prices revealed a consistently poor investment climate. Investors lost money in the average year in the 1930s, '40s and '50s, and made a small amount in the 1960s by continuously investing during this segment of the month.

The 1970s continued to be a poor time to invest during the third quarter. The apparent +0.77% increase in average annual third-quarter prices during this decade was entirely due to 1975's impressive rally when third-quarter prices rose by +16.15%. If not for 1975, the 1970s would have generated an average annual quarterly loss of -0.94% for those always invested in the third quarter.

Between 1936 and 1979, prices rose in the third quarter of January just 45% of the time.

A new trend in the 1980s

In 1980, a new third-quarter trend seems to have begun. For the first time ever, the third quarter became January's most profitable segment. Share prices rose in nine of the decade's 10 years at an average annual rate of +2.09%, one of the best performances of the entire year. The 1990s' record of three up and one down suggests that the positive third-quarter trend continues. Even better, the quarter that follows is one of the best of the entire year, giving traders two consecutive periods of above-average profit potential. Note though, that January 23rd continues to be a drain on the quarter's performance. We don't know why this is so, but the record since 1984 is three up and five down (weekends account for the missing days).

Regardless of the overall third-quarter trend, there is a way to improve the odds of making a profit. In the *1994 Investor's Diary*, we suggested that investors watch the price trend in the

Figure 2.3   **PERCENTAGE OF TIME PRICES RISE EACH TRADING DAY**

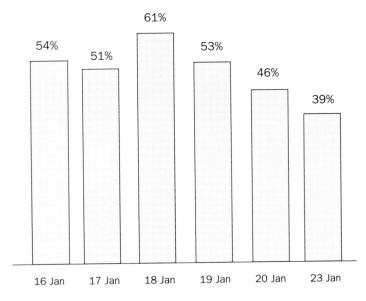

Figure 2.3: Prices tend to fall towards the end of the third quarter. Friday January 20 to Tuesday January 24 is the worst three-day stretch of the month.

first half of January. Here's a refinement of the First Half rule that will increase the odds of making a profit. If prices are up in both the first *and* second quarters of the month, by no more than +2.98% in total, the third quarter usually rises. Out of 12 such occasions since 1943, third-quarter prices rose nine times. And one of the three exceptions was a minuscule -0.07% decline in the third quarter of 1954.

An improved   *Rose (9)*
first-half rule
                     Fell (3)

Third-quarter record after a price rise in the first and second quarter of up to +2.98% in total (since 1943)

The price trend to this point of the new year also serves as a useful early warning signal for the month as a whole. This is important because the old City refrain: 'As January goes, so

As January goes, so goes the year

goes the year' is alive and well. Rising prices in January are often associated with rising prices for the next 11 months. A down January increases the odds of further declines in the rest of the year.

For investors who rely on the January price trend for insight into the direction of prices for the rest of the year, here's a tip to help you. There have been 11 occasions since records began when the first half of January *and* the third quarter both declined. On all 11 occasions, the full month finished lower. No matter how big the fourth-quarter price rise, it was never enough to compensate for the decline that had already occurred. Even more important, in eight of those 11 years, prices finished the year lower than they started.

So if you are contemplating a very long-term investment around the middle of the month, a smart course of action might be to sit tight until the situation is clarified, if the month has started off poorly.

FOURTH QUARTER OF JANUARY – JANUARY 24TH TO 31ST

Investors frequently profit during the fourth quarter of January. Between 1936–1993, prices rose 66% of the time. The average annual gain was +1.00%, second highest of all 48 quarters of the year. Only the last quarter of December, with an average annual profit of +1.05%, has out-performed it.

The fourth segment of the month failed to produce a profit in just one decade, the 1940s, when it lost -0.01% per year, equivalent to a mere one-third of a point on an FT-SE 100 in the area of 3300.

The recent fourth-quarter record has been unbelievably strong. Prices have risen in 17 of the last 20 years, and nine of the last 10, the year's best in both cases. Since the 1987 crash, prices have risen in all six years at an average of +2.68% per year.

A poor start to the quarter

Analysis of price trends on a day-by-day basis shows that the quarter starts off poorly, continuing the pattern of weakness observed at the very end of the third quarter. Prices rise just 42% of the time on January 24th (*see Figure 2.4*).

Figure 2.4

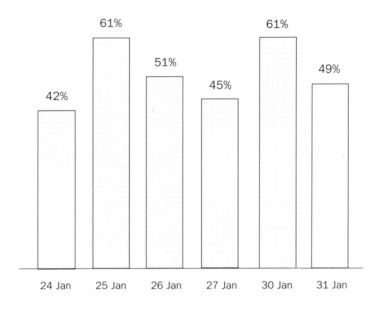

PERCENTAGE OF TIME PRICES RISE EACH TRADING DAY

Figure 2.4: The fourth quarter of January is one of the year's best quarters. But January 24th can be disappointing when it lands on a Monday or Tuesday.

Prices are also relatively weak on the very last day of the quarter, January 31st. Further analysis shows that January 31st often is profitable when it lands on a Wednesday, Thursday or Friday. But when it lands on a Monday or Tuesday, as it will do in 1995, share prices fall slightly more often than they rise.

Third-quarter signal

Here is a price signal, operative since 1936, that seems to tip off a rising price trend during the fourth quarter. If prices rise in the third quarter by a small amount, within a range of +0.41% to +0.97%, they will probably also rise in the fourth quarter.

Rose (9)

Fell (0)

Fourth-quarter record after a price rise of +0.41% to +0.97% in the third quarter

Another statistical relationship that signals an increased chance of higher prices in the fourth quarter is a rising price trend in the first half of January, followed by a decline in the third quarter. There have been 12 'up then down' occasions since 1945 and fourth-quarter prices have risen in 10 of them (83%). And in one of the two exceptional years, 1973, first half prices rose from 505.4 on the FT Ordinary Share index to 505.5, an insignificant increase of two one-hundredths of one percent.

Rose (10)

Fell (2)

Fourth-quarter record after a price rise in the first half and fall in the third quarter (since 1945)

AS JANUARY GOES, SO GOES THE YEAR

Old saws about the future direction of share prices are comforting to recite. But as investment guides, most are not to be trusted.

If you 'Sell in May and go away, and don't come back 'til St Leger's Day', you would miss being invested in the market during August, on average the year's third best investment month.

Do 'Bull Market bashes end with October crashes?' In fact, there have been more large increases in share prices during October than large decreases. Over the long-term, October has been profitable despite the headlines in 1929 and 1987.

Withstood the test of time

One exception: 'As January goes, so goes the year' has withstood the test of time for most of this century. When January share prices rise, further rises often occur in the rest of the year. Falling January prices are often associated with further declines in the remaining 11 months of the year.

But be cautious as you read articles in the financial press about this frequently-publicised price signal. A lot of what is written is either misleading or out-and-out wrong. Here are two major problem areas.

▶ Some analysts include January's performance in their yearly total, thereby loading the dice in favour of their conclusion. Predicting a full year price rise after a January price rise of 8% provides an 8% head start toward being right. It may be great for your predictive accuracy but painful for the investor who commits new funds on February 1st, based upon that advice.

A better approach is to use the January price shift to forecast the direction of prices during the 11 months that follow.

▶ The relationship between January and the rest of the year is complex. It is not simply a case of January up – rest-of-year up, or January down – rest-of-year down, as some commentators seem to suggest.

Figure 2.5   **CORRELATION BETWEEN JANUARY AND REST OF YEAR**

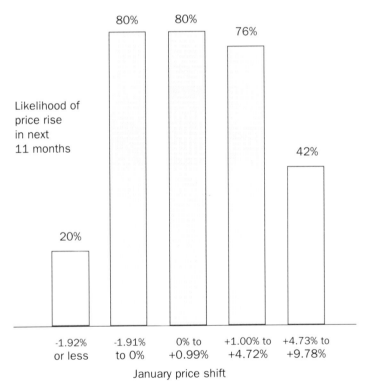

Figure 2.5: The best profit signal for the next 11 months is a January price shift within a range of -1.91% to +4.72%.

It's true that big January price declines are invariably associated with further losses in the remainder of the year. If January's prices fall by -1.92% or more, there is only a 20% chance that prices will be higher on December 31st. This level is well below average. To put that into perspective, over the long-run, prices rise 64% of the time in the February to December period.

Small losses are okay

But a small January loss is a good sign for investors, as is a small gain. Any January price move within a range of -1.91% to +4.72% is a strong signal that prices will rise in the rest of the year (*see Figure 2.5*).

The trend changes for the worse if January prices rise any higher. The odds are less than 50:50 that share prices will rise still further in the next 11 months if January prices rise +4.73% to +9.78%. Furthermore, the average level of profit for the 11 months that follows a big January price increase is just +3.66% per year, less than the level of interest provided by your neighbourhood Building Society.

There were only two years since 1919 with double-digit January price rises: +14.34% in 1989 and +51.45% in 1975. That is not enough data for us to make a proper forecast but we note that both years saw very strong further rises in the 11 months that followed.

As Table 2.4 illustrates, the January rule has been a good indicator in the recent past. It allowed us to make nine forecasts in the last 15 years. Eight were accurate. The jury is still out on the ninth.

Table 2.4   **AS JANUARY GOES, SO GOES THE YEAR (1980–1994)**

	January price shift	Rest of year (forecast)	Rest of year (actual)
1980	+8.92%	*	+14.37%
1981	-1.52%	up	+9.54%
1982	+6.29%	*	+19.90%
1983	+1.10%	up	+17.97%
1984	+6.46%	*	+21.44%
1985	+3.43%	up	+11.38%
1986	+2.02%	up	+19.77%
1987	+8.75%	*	-3.82%
1988	+5.38%	*	-0.03%
1989	+14.34%	*	+13.62%
1990	-3.15%	down	-9.80%
1991	-0.43%	up	+17.06%
1992	+3.65%	up	+9.70%
1993	-0.84%	up	+18.50%
1994	+3.90%	up	?

* No forecast in years with a January increase of +4.73% or larger

Table 2.4: The January Rule has been an accurate predictor in the recent past, correctly forecasting the direction of prices in the 11 months to follow eight times in a row. The jury is still out for 1994.

Chapter Three – February 1995

February investors always do well, except in Bull Markets and Bear Markets

Compared with the strong stock market performance of December and January, February's trend is often quite disappointing to investors. Over the long-run, the February investor would have made more money by depositing his funds in an interest-bearing savings account. Most of February's weakness occurs in the first three quarters of the month. The last quarter tends to be profitable.

Although this month is not particularly known for its volatility, a declining price trend over the last 12 months is usually associated with 100-plus point swings on the FT-SE 100. There are several historic price trends which tip off in which direction that swing will go.

A review of all February's closing prices since 1919 reveals a basic trend which has held firm for three-quarters of this century – investors who hold shares every February, for the entire month, are making a poor investment decision. A February investor is better off placing his money into a savings account, gaining a higher average return on capital, with no risk to boot.

According to one City wag, there are just two kinds of markets where February prices are especially likely to be weak – Bull Markets and Bear Markets!

This light-hearted advice is remarkably accurate. Between 1919 and 1993, February's shares prices rose just 49% of the time. In contrast, January prices rose 72% of the time. In relative terms, that's 47% more often.

Zero profits

During this period, the average February share price rise was just +0.31% per year, equal to 10 points on an FT-SE 100 of 3300. A hypothetical investor who only invested in February, from 1919 to 1993, would have run up his £1,000 to just £1,138. If the explosive rally of 1975, which signalled the end of the 1973–74 Bear Market, was eliminated from these computations (February prices rose +23.28%), investors would have obtained a 0.00% return after 74 years of steady investing. Historically, February is ranked seventh on monthly profitability. Without 1975, its rank would drop to ninth position.

Although profits were gained in some years, the long-term February investor lost money in the 1930s, '40s, '50s, and '60s. The large average annual increase of the 1970s was almost entirely due to 1975. In the 1980s' Bull Market, February performed better than its long-term average, as did most other months, producing an average annual monthly gain of +2.05%. But since October, 1987, February has reverted to traditional form with a record of three ups and three downs (*see Table 3.1*).

The Three-Year rule

The best-ever stretch of time for the February investor was back in 1922–5 when shares rose in value in four consecutive years. Since then there have been three occasions when prices rose three years in a row: 1944–6, 1979–81 and 1991–3. Each time, they fell the following year. In the most recent assault on the Three-Year rule, share prices rose to new peaks in December, 1993 and January, 1994 as commentators repeatedly warned that the stock market was over-extended and ripe for a fall. But prices kept rising until the start of February when they suddenly ran out of steam with a -3% setback.

Incidentally, in the single exception to the Three-Year rule, the four year up-turn of 1922–25, February share prices rose by just +0.51% in 1925. It seems safe to assume that any long-term change in the February trend will be associated with a successful attack on the Three-Year rule. Until then, invest in February with caution.

Why are share prices so disappointing in February? No one knows with any certainty. Obviously, no market can continue

Table 3.1   **FEBRUARY PRICE RISES AND DECLINES: 1919–1993**

	Average February price change	Up	Down
1920–29	1.06%	7	3
1930–39	-0.11%	4	6
1940–49	-1.93%	4	6
1950–59	-0.80%	6	4
1960–69	-1.05%	3	7
1970–79	2.40%	5	5
1980–89	2.05%	5	5
1990–93	2.43%	3	1
Average February price change	0.31%	37	38

Table 3.1: Historically, February has been a poor month in which to invest. Without 1975's rise of +23.28%, the 1970–79 average price rise was just +0.08%, equal to about three points on an FT-SE 100 of 3300 and the 74-year average would be exactly even (0.00%). The apparent improvement in the 1980s was a Bull Market phenomenon. Since the 1987 crash, the February record is three up and three down.

to rise forever. Prices must rest or occasionally react against a rising up-trend in even the best Bull Market. But why does it happen so consistently in February? Why not in January? Why not in December? One guess is that the of start-of-year money flows and up-to-the-minute company statements which often powers a January price advance peters out in February.

Fourth quarter is profitable

Despite the poor overall trend, there are a number of ways to profit with a February investment. Take, for example, the pattern of profit and loss during different parts of the month. Over the long-term, virtually all of February's profits have been realised in the last week of the month which rises 60% of the time. This pattern of fourth quarter strength has been operative for many decades. The last week of the month has been either first or second-ranked from the 1930s to the 1970s. It is the fifth-best quarter of the entire year.

At first glance, the profit picture seems to have changed in the 1980s when fourth-quarter profits were surpassed by the first and second quarters. In fact, what happened was that the

Table 3.2

PERCENTAGE PRICE CHANGE: FEBRUARY 1936–1993

	February 1–7	February 8–14	February 15–21	February 22–28(9)
Average annual price change				
1936–39	0.30%	-0.43%	0.07%	1.51%
1940–49	-0.74%	-1.17%	-0.30%	0.39%
1950–59	0.81%	-0.83%	-0.73%	-0.02%
1960–69	-0.32%	0.15%	-0.88%	-0.25%
1970–79	-0.56%	-0.43%	0.03%	3.05%
1980–89	0.94%	0.97%	-0.02%	0.62%
1990–93	0.18%	0.55%	0.40%	0.95%
Average quarterly price change	0.06%	-0.22%	-0.30%	0.82%
Number of years in which prices:				
rose	26	26	26	35
fell	28	32	31	22
remained unchanged	4	–	1	1

Table 3.2: Most February profits are gained in the fourth quarter. Without 1975. the average quarterly price change would be: first quarter: -0.09%; second quarter: -0.35%; third quarter: -0.21%; fourth quarter: +0.56%. In most years, the best strategy is to stand aside until the end of the month.

first and second quarters improved a lot during the 1980s' Bull Market. After the 1987 crash, the long-term strength of the fourth quarter again became apparent (*see Table 3.2*).

Profit opportunity   One way to beat the odds in February is to identify specific years when share prices are especially likely to rise or decline. One trend which, historically, has done a good job of anticipating the direction of February price shifts is the price trend in the past year. If prices shift within the following limits, the odds of a February profit is quite high.[1]

[1] Reminder: All monthly calculations are based on the FT-Non-Financial Index, formerly the FT-'500'; unless otherwise stated, they are based on data from 1919–1993. All daily, quarterly, and bi-monthly calculations are based on the Ordinary Share Index, also known as the FT-30; unless otherwise stated, they are based on data from 1936–1993.

Previous 12 months: price shift between -4.40% to +13.63%
Previous 6 months: price shift between -2.21% to +11.79%
Previous 3 months: price rise (any amount)
Previous month: price rise between +0.07% to +9.78%

Since 1920, there have been 14 years with price shifts within these limits in the run-up to February. February prices rose in 13 of those years. The single exception was back in 1929.

Rose (13)

Fell (1)

February record if prices shift within defined limits (since 1920)

The average annual February profit in these 14 years was a quite healthy +2.36%. But one word of warning. Watch the size of the past 12 month up-move very carefully. If price rise by more than +13.63%, the probability of a decline in February increases sharply.

Watch prices in prior three months

A second trend to watch for is the direction of prices in November to January. There have been 10 instances where prices rose in the past three months between +1.72% and +3.07%. February prices rose in all 10 years. The average annual increase was +3.17%.

Rose (10)

Fell (0)

February record after a price rise of +1.72% to +3.07% in November to January

If we eliminate duplication within these two trends, there were 18 years that were flagged by at least one of them. February prices rose 17 times. In the remaining 56 years between 1920 and 1993, February's record was simply terrible. Prices fell 64% of the time (20 up and 36 down).

In the *1994 Investor's Diary*, we advised investors of a relationship between the second half of January and the month of February Here is a refinement of that trend that will increase the odds of a profit. If prices decline in January's second half by no more than -3.30%, there is a strong likelihood that prices will fall in February. Out of 20 falls in this range, February prices fell 16 times.

The January
second-half signal

Rose (4)

Fell (16)

February record after prices fell up to -3.30% in January's second half (since 1936)

Although its long-term record is poor, February prices are not particularly volatile. Shifts of + or -3.03% or more (at least 100 points on an FT-SE 100 of 3300) are about average compared with other months. But if prices have dropped in the past 12 months by at least -3.68%, be on the alert for very volatile trading conditions.

Since 1920, there have been 22 years in which share prices declined by at least -3.68% in the 12 months preceding February. February's prices rose or fell by at least 3% in 18 of those years. And two of the four smaller moves were near misses. With moves of this magnitude, it is important to know the direction of the shift so that you can either step aside or commit more funds for a short-term investment. In addition to the forecasting tools described earlier, the stock market provides one other clue – the direction of prices in the first quarter of February.

Watch for Big
Move signals

Since 1936, there were 17 Big Move signals (past 12 months down by -3.68% or worse). In 14 of those years, the direction that prices shifted in the first quarter were followed by further shifts in the same direction during the rest of the month. It's not a perfect answer since part of the move has already occurred. But knowing that three-quarters of a Big Move is still to come is a whole lot better than having no information at all.

FIRST QUARTER OF FEBRUARY – FEBRUARY 1ST TO FEBRUARY 7TH

It's tough to turn a profit in February by steadily holding shares year-in and year-out. Profiting in the first quarter of the month is even more difficult.

The general investment climate is poor. The average increase in share prices during the first quarter is just +0.06% per year, equal to about two points on a 3300 FT-SE 100. If we eliminate all profits associated with 1975, an annual investment in February's first quarter would produce a loss. Profits seem to have improved since 1980 but this is a function of the Bull Market which saw many segments of the year perform better than their long-term average. Since the 1987 crash, the first-quarter record has reverted to form – three up and three down.

Invest selectively to profit

Nevertheless, it is possible to profit in this difficult time period by investing selectively. One key period to watch is the direction that prices move during the month of January. Since 1965, each time January's prices rose by +3.65% to +8.33%, they fell in the first quarter of February.

Rose (0)

Fell (9)

First-quarter record after a price rise of +3.65% to +8.33% in January (since 1965)

Another period to watch is the direction of prices in the last half of January. If prices increase by +1.27% to +2.63%, there is a very good chance of a price rise in the first quarter of February.

Rose (10)

Fell (0)

First-quarter record after a price rise of +1.27% to +2.63% in January's second half

A price decline in January's second half also sends a useful forecasting signal. Since 1967, the price of an average share fell nine times in the last half of January. Prices continued to disappoint in the first quarter of February in all nine years (eight declines and one no change). Betting against the market (eg, buying Puts) or simply pulling out completely, would have been a profitable course of action to take during these nine years.

Rose (0)

Fell (8)

No change (1)

First-quarter record after a price decline in January's second half (since 1967)

A strange correlation

In the *1994 Investor's Diary*, we reported on a strange correlation between the third quarter of January and February's first quarter. It seems that a drop in prices during January's third quarter is often followed by a price decline in the first quarter of February, regardless of how prices move in January's fourth quarter. Apparently, market forces and money flows during January's fourth quarter (one of the best quarters of the entire year) are sufficiently powerful to overwhelm the negative trend for a short period of time. But, as soon as the fourth quarter ends, the negative trend comes back into effect at the beginning of February.

Here is an update on that trend that will increase the chance of making a profit. Since 1960, prices fell in January's third quarter by -0.87% or more in ten different years. Prices continued to decline in each of these years in the first quarter of February, regardless of how they moved in January's fourth quarter.

Rose (0)

Fell (10)

First-quarter record after a price fall of -0.87% or more in January's third quarter (since 1960)

In the remaining 24 years since 1960, prices fell in February's first quarter just eight times (33%). Had you invested in shares only on occasions preceded by an increase in January's third quarter, or by a small fall of less than -0.87%, you would have realised an average first-quarter gain of +0.96%.

Rose (16)

Fell (8)

First-quarter record after a price rise in January's third quarter or decline of less than -0.87% (since 1960)

First two days are best

If you plan to purchase any shares during this quarter of the month, keep in mind that the first two days are the most profitable. The three trading days that follow lose money in most years. The clear implication to investors: if you are planning to invest new funds from the 3rd onward, in most years it would pay you to keep your money in a bank; if you are planning to sell, the odds favour holding on for the first two days of the quarter. Following this strategy will not increase your profits each and every year but will shade things a bit more in your favour over the long-run (*see Figure 3.1*).

SECOND QUARTER OF FEBRUARY – FEBRUARY 8TH TO 14TH

February's second quarter is another tough period within which to make money in the stock market. Prices fall 55% of the time and generate an average annual loss of -0.22%.

The investment climate seems to have improved in the 1980s. Prices rose six times, fell four times, and increased at an average rate of +0.97%. But here again, the improvement was a temporary Bull Market phenomenon. The trend since 1987 has reverted to form with a record of two up and four down (*see Table 3.3*).

The stock market does, however, send several key signals that help nimble investors to profit or avoid losses during these

Figure 3.1

PERCENTAGE OF TIME PRICES RISE EACH TRADING DAY IN FEBRUARY'S FIRST QUARTER

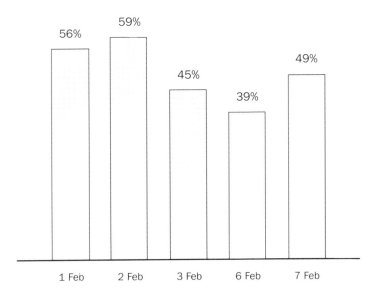

Figure 3.1: The first two days are the best days of the quarter. If you are planning to sell shares around this point of the year, the odds suggest holding on during these two days.

very difficult trading conditions. One signal to watch for is a flat price trend in January's third quarter. If possible, avoid holding shares when this signal flashes as it correlates with further weakness in mid-February. By a 'flat' price trend, we mean any small shift within a range of -0.52% to +0.43%. Between 1936–1993, there were 14 years with small third-quarter price shifts within this range. February's second quarter fell in 12 of those years (86% of the time) and generated an average loss of -1.51% per year.

Rose (2)

Fell (12)

Second-quarter record after a price shift of -0.52% to +0.43% in January's third quarter

Table 3.3

PERCENTAGE PRICE CHANGE FOR FEBRUARY SINCE 1980

	February 1–7	February 8–14	February 15–21	February 24–28 (9)
1980	2.12%	2.38%	-3.44%	2.08%
1981	3.00%	2.69%	-0.97%	3.73%
1982	-0.29%	-1.31%	-1.44%	-2.67%
1983	3.26%	2.75%	-2.44%	-1.07%
1984	-3.81%	1.55%	0.89%	0.06%
1985	0.31%	-0.45%	0.02%	-0.39%
1986	2.30%	2.62%	3.05%	1.70%
1987	4.71%	0.80%	3.02%	2.09%
1988	-3.39%	-0.15%	-0.17%	3.39%
1989	1.22%	-1.17%	1.25%	-2.71%
1990	-2.03%	-0.21%	-2.12%	-0.13%
1991	3.43%	3.49%	1.49%	3.58%
1992	-2.58%	0.30%	1.64%	0.01%
1993	1.90%	-1.40%	0.60%	0.35%
Average quarterly price change				
1980–89	0.94%	0.97%	-0.02%	0.62%
1980–93	0.73%	0.85%	0.10%	0.72%
Number of years in which prices:				
rose	9	8	8	9
fell	5	6	6	5

Table 3.3: The first- and second-quarter trend improved during the 1980s. Alas, it was a Bull Market phenomenon. Since the 1987 crash, both quarters returned to traditional, less profitable trading patterns.

The first-quarter signal

Another price signal to watch is the direction of prices in February's first quarter. If they fall slightly, by -0.29% to -1.01%, share prices will probably also drop in the second quarter. Out of 11 declines of this magnitude in the first quarter, second-quarter prices dropped 10 times. The average decline was -0.98% per year, about 32 points on an FT-SE 100 in the area of 3300.

Rose (1) ☐

Fell (10) ☐

Second-quarter record after a price fall of -0.29% to -1.01% in the first quarter

If we eliminate duplication within these two trends, there are 21 years that are flagged by at least one of them. Second-quarter prices fell 18 times. In the remaining 37 years since 1936, the first-quarter record was up 23 and down 14. You wouldn't make money every year but simply avoiding share ownership when warned would lead to a small average annual profit during the years that you did invest.

The best trading day of the quarter

As you execute your trades, keep in mind that the very best trading day in this quarter is February 13th when prices rise 54% of the time (*see Figure 3.2*). During the last 20 years, prices have been especially strong on this day, rising in 11 out of 15 years (Saturdays and Sundays account for the missing days). Unfortunately history also reveals a persistent weakness in share price on the second Monday of February. The 13th of the month has landed on a Monday eight times since 1936. Prices rose once. Before dismissing this as an interesting, but statistically untrustworthy observation because of the low number of observations, consider this: The 12th also landed on a Monday in eight years and rose just twice. And the 14th rose on a Monday in just one year out of nine. In general, daily prices rise 48% of the time during the month of February. They rise 38% of the time on February Mondays. Within this context, a 16% rate of increase for Monday, the 12th, 13th and 14th seems excessively low.

Watch mid-month Mondays

Here is the record for every Monday, February 12, 13 and 14 since 1970:

	One-day price shift		One day price shift
14 Feb 1972	-1.73%	14 Feb 1983	-0.27%
12 Feb 1973	-0.13%	13 Feb 1984	-0.30%
14 Feb 1977	-3.98%	13 Feb 1989	-1.36%
13 Feb 1978	-0.23%	12 Feb 1990	-1.10%
12 Feb 1979	-1.02%		

Figure 3.2

PERCENTAGE OF TIME PRICES RISE EACH TRADING DAY IN FEBRUARY'S SECOND QUARTER

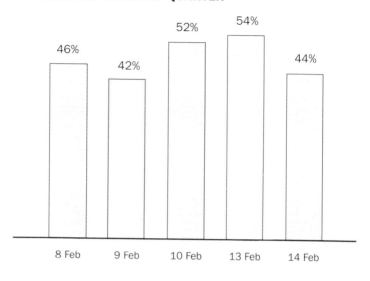

Figure 3.2: February 13th is the best day of the quarter. But prices have a strong tendency to fall when February 13th lands on a Monday.

In case you haven't noticed, February 13th lands on a Monday in 1995.

St Valentine's Day   Incidentally, February 14th, St. Valentine's Day, is disappointing to investors, even when it does not land on a Monday. On average, prices rise just 44% of the time. If you have ever wondered why Cupid is always shooting arrows at people, perhaps it is because he's a frustrated investor!

THIRD QUARTER OF FEBRUARY – FEBRUARY 15TH TO FEBRUARY 21ST

The third quarter of February has been a money-loser since the 1940s. The typical share price fell 53% of the time between 1936 and 1993, with an average decline of -0.30%. Even during the 1980s when other so-so segments of the year turned a profit, the third quarter was a money-loser. But the trend has improved in recent years, an event we shall monitor with great interest.

Odds favour mid-month Thursdays for up-moves

The best days of the quarter are the 15th and 17th. The 16th looks to be the weak link between the two, with a 44% likelihood of rising, but shares seem to do well on mid-month Thursdays. Since 1936, prices rise 69% of the time whenever February 14–17 lands on a Thursday. No guarantees of course, but February 16 lands on a Thursday in 1995 so the odds favour an up-move.

Unfortunately, the price trend soon weakens. The 21st is one of the weakest days of the entire year. Prices rise just 29% of the time (*see Figure 3.3*).

If you are planning to sell shares during this quarter, in most years the odds suggest the transaction should be completed before the 20th arrives. And keep in mind that the best way to consistently profit in this quarter is either to deposit your funds in an interest-bearing account or to bet against the market, despite the strength at the beginning of the quarter.

If you choose to bet on a falling market, here are some pointers to help you to increase the probability of profiting:

First-half price signal

▶ Keep on the look out for weak prices in the first half of February. If the first quarter rises by no more than +0.61%, or falls by any amount, and the second quarter falls by -0.74% to -2.62%, the third quarter is especially likely to fall. The average annual decline during these years is -1.79%

Rose (0)

Fell (10)

Third-quarter record after a price shift of +0.61% or less in first quarter and a decline of -0.74% to -2.62% in second quarter

Figure 3.3

PERCENTAGE OF TIME PRICES RISE EACH TRADING DAY IN FEBRUARY'S THIRD QUARTER

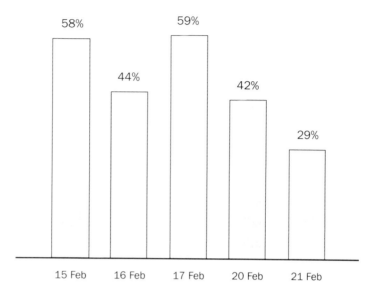

Figure 3.3: Share prices often rise on February 16th if it lands on a Thursday, so the odds favour investors in 1995. But the trend soon deteriorates. February 21st is one of the worst trading days of the entire year.

▶ An even better early warning signal is a weak price trend in January's second half *and* February's first half. If prices decline in February's first half and either rise by no more than +0.33% or decline in January's second half, they will almost certainly decline in the third quarter. Between 1936 and 1993, there were 19 years that fit this profile. The third quarter of February declined in 18 of those years (95%). The single exception was back in 1947. The average decline was -1.41% per year.

Rose (1)

Fell (18)

Third-quarter record after a price shift of +0.33% or less in January's second half and a decline in February's first half

In the midst of all this carnage, there is one price trend that consistently forecasts rising prices in this quarter – a small shift in prices during the first half of the month. If prices shift slightly in the first half, by -0.14% to +1.15%, there is a 91% chance that third-quarter prices will also rise. The single exception to the rule occurred in 1967.

Rose (10)

Fell (1)

Third-quarter record after a price shift of -0.14% to +1.15% in first half

FOURTH QUARTER OF FEBRUARY – FEBRUARY 22ND TO FEBRUARY 28TH

Strong day

The fourth quarter is February's best segment. Prices rise 60% of the time. It is February's only quarterly segment that rises in most years. Between 1936 and 1993, the average annual gain was +0.82%.

The two most profitable consecutive trading days in the quarter are the last two. In fact, February 28th is the best day of the month – prices rise 63% of the time. So if you are planning to sell shares late in the month, the odds favour holding on until the very end of the month (*see Figure 3.4*).

In most years, February 28th is a very safe day in which to hold shares. In addition to the high percentage of time that prices rise, it is one of the few days in the entire year in which prices have never fallen by over 1%.

Weak day

In contrast, February 23rd is the quarter's weakest link. Prices have risen just 42% of the time since 1936. And the recent trend shows no sign of improvement. In the last 10 years, the February 23rd record is one up and five down.

If you want to improve the odds of making a profit during the fourth quarter, watch the behaviour of prices in the two preceding quarters. We first called this relationship to the attention of readers in the *1994 Investor's Diary*. Here is an update which increases the odds of a fourth-quarter profit.

Figure 3.4

PERCENTAGE OF TIME PRICES RISE EACH TRADING DAY IN FEBRUARY'S FOURTH QUARTER

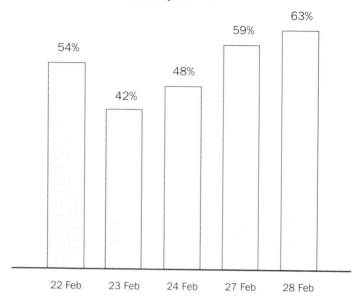

Figure 3.4: February 28th is the best day of the month. If you plan to sell shares near the end of the month, holding on until the very end will move profits a bit more in your favour in most years.

Between 1936 and 1993 there were 15 occasions when share prices rose by at least +1.69% in total in the second and third quarters. Prices continued to rise in the fourth quarter in 13 of those years (87%). The average increase was +2.52%.

Rose (13)

Fell (2)

Fourth-quarter record after a price rise of at least +1.69% in the second and third quarters

There is also a relationship between the first half of February and the fourth quarter, regardless of which direction prices move in the third quarter. If the first-half price trend rises by at least +1.15%, there is a very high likelihood it will also rise in the fourth quarter. Since 1936, first-half prices rose by this level 18 times. Fourth-quarter prices also rose in 16 of those years (89%). The average annual increase was +2.24%

First-half price
signal

Rose (16)

Fell (2)

Fourth-quarter record after a price rise of at least +1.15% in the first half

Here's one final statistical relationship to help you to make money in February. We offer no rationale to explain why it works. But it does work. Since 1956, there have been 10 leap years. Fourth-quarter prices have risen in every single one of them. The average annual price increase was +1.62%. During the other 28 years since 1956, fourth-quarter prices have risen just 44% of the time.

Surprisingly, February 29th itself is not consistently profitable. Since 1956, its record is three up and four down (the missing three days fell on weekends) with an average daily loss of -0.26%.

Chapter Four – March 1995

> Budget Day has been moved to late November. Too bad for the March investor. Without Budget Day to help things along, there is a danger that the March trend will return to historic, lacklustre levels last seen in the 1920s, '30s and '40s. Fortunately, there are several signals that tip off many of this month's profits and losses.

Investors who held shares every March made very little money. Between 1919 and 1993, March prices rose 56% of the time. The average price rise was just 0.69%, equal to 23 points on an FT-SE 100 in the area of 3300. Historically, March has been the sixth-best month to invest in shares (*see Table 4.1*). A 1919 investment of £1,000, held in shares each March and in cash for the other 11 months of the year, would now be worth just £1,512 after 75 years of steady investing.

Table 4.1

MARCH PRICE RISES AND DECLINES: 1919–1993

	Average March price change	Up	Down
1920–29	0.59%	4	6
1930–39	-0.40%	4	6
1940–49	-0.62%	3	7
1950–59	0.40%	7	3
1960–69	2.25%	7	3
1970–79	-0.33%	6	4
1980–89	2.11%	8	2
1990–93	-0.08%	2	2
Average March price change	0.69%	42	33

Table 4.1: The March record has steadily improved in the last few decades. The loss in the 1970s was due to back-to-back disasters in 1974 and 1975 of -19.55% and -13.44%. The fact that the average loss for the decade as a whole was just -0.33% speaks for the market's strength in the rest of the decade (up six and down two).

But a peek under the surface reveals a steady improvement in March's performance. From 1919–43, the first 25 years of our historical record, March prices rose just 10 times. In the next 25 years, they rose 15 times. And from 1969 to 1993, they rose 17 times.

Good results despite 1974 and 1975

The monthly trend was profitable in 1969–93 despite two very atypical years. In 1974, March was slammed by a -19.55% drop, the worst monthly drop in the entire 1973–4 Bear Market, and the third-worst month of all time. Only October 1987 (-26.21%) and June 1940 (-22.10%), when investors feared we might lose the war, were worse. In 1975, March gave back some of the profits rung up in the explosive January/February rally marking the end of the 1973–4 Bear Market, with a drop of -13.44%. March has the dubious distinction of being the only month of the year with two entries in the list of the 10 worst months of all time (see Table 4.2).

Table 4.2

TEN WORST MONTHS IN HISTORY

	Percentage decline
October 1987	-26.21%
June 1940	-22.10%
March 1974	-19.55%
August 1947	-17.04%
September 1981	-16.94%
April 1920	-15.75%
November 1974	-15.67%
March 1975	-13.44%
February 1948	-13.18%
July 1966	-13.00%

Table 4.2: The worst month in history was October 1987, when prices fell by -26.21%. Some commentators call October/November 1987 history's only two-month long Bear Market (prices fell another -10.28% in November). In fact, the market actually peaked in mid-July 1987. Still, the carnage was even worse than in June 1940, when many thought we might lose the war and ran for cover.

Figure 4.1

NUMBER OF TIMES MARCH PRICES ROSE: 1919–1993

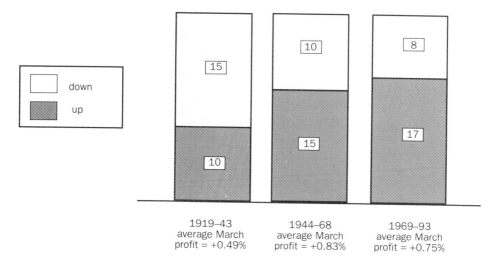

□ down

▨ up

1919–43	1944–68	1969–93
average March	average March	average March
profit = +0.49%	profit = +0.83%	profit = +0.75%

Figure 4.1: March prices rose more frequently in successive 25-year periods. So did profitability. The average annual profit of +0.75% in 1969–93 would have been a much higher +2.25% if not for 1974 and 1975.

Even with these two years included, investors turned an average annual profit with a steady March investment during the 1969 –93 time period. Without them, March's performance would have shown a considerable improvement over the previous 25 year period (*see Figure 4.1*).

Budget Day affects March trends

Budget Day seems to play a role in March's long-term performance. In the money-losing 1919–43 period, 21 out of 25 budgets were presented in late April. The date was often scheduled in early/mid-April in the next 25 year period, and March profits rose. By 1969–93, just two budgets were presented in late April while 19 were presented in March and March's typical profits improved once again, a fact hidden by the twin horrors of 1974 and 1975. It's probably no coincidence that the Budget Day trend and the March profit trend are so similar (*see Figure 4.2*).

March was exceptionally good to investors during the 1980s, turning in its best ever decade (as did other months). Prices rose in eight out of 10 years. The average monthly price

Figure 4.2   **MARCH PROFITS AND BUDGET DAY: 1919–1993**

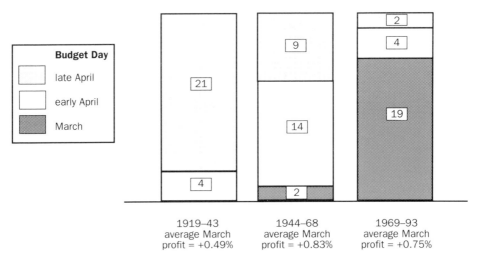

Budget Day	
☐	late April
☐	early April
▨	March

1919–43
average March
profit = +0.49%

1944–68
average March
profit = +0.83%

1969–93
average March
profit = +0.75%

Figure 4.2: March profitability improved in line with earlier Budget Days. In 1919 to 1943, most Budget Days were in late-April and March profits were relatively low. In the last few decades, there were just two late-April budgets and 19 March budgets. Average annual profits were high despite the twin horrors of 1974–75.

First half vs. second half

rise was +2.11%. As this fine performance was heavily influenced by the Bull Market as well as the shift to March budgets, we caution readers not to extrapolate this trend into the future.

Budget Day affects the point in the month when most profits are accumulated, as well as the month's overall performance. Prior to 1970, second-half prices rose 68% of the time as against 32% in the first half. Since then, as the tendency for Budget Days to be presented in the first half of March became more pronounced, the profit pattern abruptly changed. Second-half prices rose just 37% of the time, producing an average loss of -0.74%. The second half became a time period to avoid unless you were betting on the down-side. The recent second-half trend has been worsening. Prices fell in six of the past seven years.

Meanwhile, the strength formerly associated with the second half has shifted to the first half. First-half prices have risen 71% of the time since 1970 compared to 32% pre-1970. The average profit since 1970 is +1.38% (*see Figure 4.3*).

Figure 4.3

PERCENTAGE OF TIME PRICES RISE AND FALL EACH HALF OF MARCH: 1936–1993

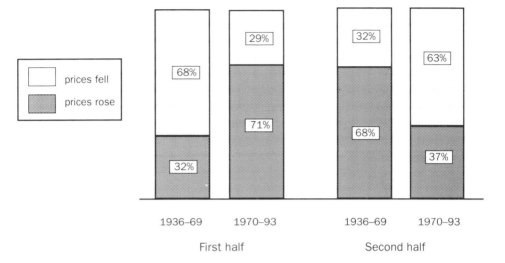

Figure 4.3: The shift to a mid-March budget in the 1970s had a strong and immediate effect on the pattern of profits in the first-versus-second half of the month. The first half of March became the most profitable part of the month.

How will March prices behave now that March budgets are a thing of the past? No one knows for sure. The answer will become clear in two or three decades from now. For the present, consider this:

▶ From 1919 to 1943, when most budgets were presented in late April, and March business news contained little coverage of the up-coming budget, March was a mediocre month.

▶ From 1944 to 1968, when budgets were often presented in the first half of April, the second half of March was much more profitable than the first half. Although the third and fourth quarters rose the same amount of time during this period, the fourth quarter, one week closer to Budget Day, tended to generate bigger increases.

Figure 4.4   **PERCENTAGE OF TIME PRICES RISE EACH QUARTER OF MARCH: 1936–1993**

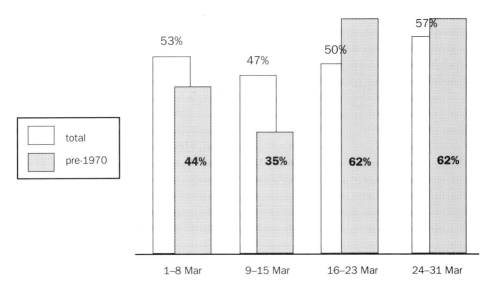

Figure 4.4: The first half of March used to be quite painful to investors, especially the second quarter. Prices fell in two out of three years. The trend improved with the advent of March budgets. Look out for possible trouble now that March budgets are a thing of the past.

▶ During the 1980s, a period of tax cuts and generally well-received budgets, most budgets were presented around the middle of March. The first and second quarters of the month became March's most profitable segments.

Weaker prices

Our hypothesis is for a return to poor March trading conditions, now that Budget Day no longer affects March prices. The relationship is clearly indicated in Figure 4.4 which shows just how poorly the first and second quarters used to perform, especially the second quarter, before most budgets were presented in March

As with other months, historical price trends help to identify specific years when March prices are especially likely to rise or decline. Unfortunately, the effect of the Budget Day shift adds an unknown dimension to these forecasts as far as March is concerned. Here are several trends which, historically, have done a good job of anticipating the direction of March price shifts and which we believe are the least dependent on Budget Day. We will not know for certain if our hypothesis is correct for several more years.[1]

12-month indicator

The direction of prices during the preceding March 1st to February 28th has traditionally been a good predictor of March prices. Big rises in the preceding 12 months are often associated with a March profit. Since 1953, there have been 16 years in which prices rose between +10.27% to +35.45% in the preceding 12 months. March shares rose each time. Since this trend was operative prior to the 1970s, as well as more recently, we believe it is still operative today.

Rose (16)

Fell (0)

March record after a price rise of +10.27% to +35.45% in the 12 preceding months (since 1953)

Three-month indicator

Another signal to look for is a price decline in December to February. A small price decline in this period is often associated with further declines in March. A large decline is often associated with rising March prices. The magic number to watch for is a decline of about -3%. Better than that is a danger signal.

Here is the evidence: there have been 12 instances where prices fell in the past three months within a range of -3.30% and -13.71%. March prices rose in 10 of those years. The two exceptions were in 1952 and 1974.

Rose (10)

Fell (2)

March record after a price fall of -3.30% to -13.71% in the three preceding months

---

[1] Reminder: All monthly calculations are based on the FT-Non-Financial Index, formerly the FT-'500'; unless otherwise stated, they are based on data from 1919–1993. All daily, quarterly, and bi-monthly calculations are based on the Ordinary Share Index, also known as the FT-30; unless otherwise stated, they are based on data from 1936–1993.

There were 13 other years with smaller price declines during December to February, within a range of -0.39% to -2.99%. The March record during these 13 years was up twice and down 11 times. The last exception was in 1981.

Rose (2)

Fell (11)

March record after a price fall of -0.39%to -2.99% in the three preceding months

Watch February's fourth quarter

Readers of the *1994 Investor's Diary* may recall our observation that the direction of prices in the fourth quarter of February often tips off the direction of March price shifts. Here is an update on that trend which may increase the likelihood of profit. A small fourth-quarter move on the up-side, within a range of +0.44% to +1.70%, often signals an increase in March share prices. Since 1936, there have been 11 quarterly shifts of that size. March prices rose in nine of those years with an average annual increase of +2.86%.

Rose (9)

Fell (2)

March record after a price rise of +0.44% to +1.70% in February's fourth quarter

We also reported last year that if share prices fall in February's fourth quarter, the odds are good that March prices will rise. In effect, the failure of prices to rise in February's best quarter often transfers positive price pressure to March. Here's an update. There have been nine occasions since 1967 when February's fourth quarter declined by -0.39% or more. March prices rose in each of those years, with an average annual increase of +3.78%.

Rose (9) [   ]

Fell (0) |

March record after a price fall of -0.39% or more in February's
fourth quarter (since 1967)

While this trend has been an extremely accurate predictor in the
past, and our update sharpens things even further, note that it
has come into effect in 1967, around the time that Budget Day's
effect on March prices became most pronounced. For this
reason, we recommend readers use this trend cautiously until it
can prove itself in the new March climate.

FIRST QUARTER OF MARCH – MARCH 1ST TO 8TH

Like the month as a whole, investors gained very little by
steadily investing every first quarter of March. After 58 years,
the first quarter produced a record of 31 up, 27 down and a
+0.08% level of price increase. That would be the equivalent of
less than three points a year on a 3300 FT-SE 100.

March budgets helped the first quarter

A decade-by-decade analysis finds small up or down price
movements during the 1930s and '40s, when budgets were
often presented in late April, and the 1950s and '60s, when
budgets were often presented in early or mid-April. Once
budgets were moved to March, there was a marked improvement in the first-quarter trend. The relatively large average
annual decline of -1.06% in the 1970s was largely due to a
-12.67% decline in the 1974 Bear Market. Prices rose throughout the remainder of the decade and continued to do so in the
1980s with rises in eight out of ten years and an average annual
gain of +1.33% (*see Table 4.3*).

Poor trading conditions

With March budgets a thing of the past, we fear a return to
poor trading conditions during this quarter of the month. Our
view of the future is quite visible in Figure 4.5 which shows daily
price changes for the quarter over the long-run. Without the
stimulus provided by the strong performance of the last two
decades, the daily trend for first-quarter share prices is decidedly

Table 4.3 **PERCENTAGE PRICE CHANGE: MARCH 1936–1993**

	March 1–8	March 9–15	March 16–23	March 24–31
Average annual price change				
1936–39	-0.57%	-2.89%	0.24%	-0.96%
1940–49	-0.40%	-0.63%	0.12%	0.43%
1950–59	0.02%	-0.76%	0.67%	0.61%
1960–69	0.19%	0.39%	0.51%	0.82%
1970–79	-1.06%	1.92%	-1.02%	0.19%
1980–89	1.33%	0.72%	0.21%	-0.71%
1990–93	1.51%	-0.48%	-0.74%	-0.34%
Average quarterly price change	0.08%	0.05%	0.05%	0.14%
Number of years in which prices:				
rose	31	27	29	33
fell	27	30	28	24
remained unchanged	–	1	1	1

Table 4.3: The first- and second-quarter profit trend improved with the shift to a March budget. The first-quarter improvement is disguised by the drop of -12.67% in 1974. Both quarters could revert to former weakness now that March budgets are a thing of the past.

---

mediocre. Prices fell in the majority of all days except one.

The chronic Budget Day shifts make trend-spotting especially hazardous during this part of the year. But three trends have been in effect since before World War II, pre-dating the effects of March Budget Days: one of them is the direction of prices during the month of February. If they fluctuate by a small amount, from -1.35% to +1.15%, it is likely that first-quarter prices will rise. Since 1936, there have been 13 years with a small February move within this range. First-quarter prices rose in 11 of them (85%).

Figure 4.5

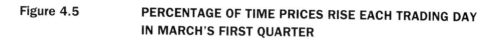

PERCENTAGE OF TIME PRICES RISE EACH TRADING DAY IN MARCH'S FIRST QUARTER

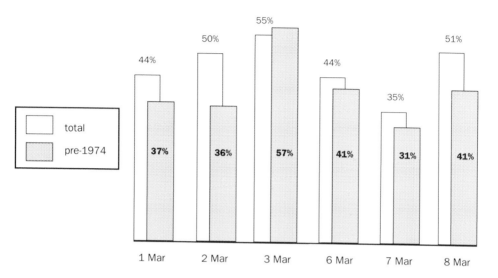

Figure 4.5: Prior to 1974, prices fell most of the time in the first quarter. The disparity is especially large on March 2nd.

Rose (11)

Fell (2)

First-quarter record after a price shift of -1.35% to +1.15% in February

The February fourth-quarter signal

The direction that prices move in February's fourth quarter also helps investors to anticipate the first-quarter trend. If prices decline in February's fourth quarter within a range of -0.70% to -2.71%, the chances are good they will rise strongly in the first quarter of March. Between 1936 and 1993, February's fourth quarter declined 15 times within this range. March's first quarter rose in 13 of those years (87%) at an average annual rate of +1.56%.

Rose (13)

Fell (2)

First-quarter record after a price fall of -0.70% to -2.71% in February's fourth quarter

Just as a small decline in February's fourth quarter often forecasts a price rise in the first quarter, a small rise often signals a first-quarter decline. Out of 10 years with small February fourth-quarter price rises in the range of +0.42% to +1.34%, March prices fell nine times, at an average annual rate of -1.57%.

Rose (1)

Fell (9)

First-quarter record after a price rise of +0.42% to +1.34% in February's fourth quarter

SECOND QUARTER OF MARCH – MARCH 9TH TO MARCH 15TH

Second-quarter prices rose 47% of the time between 1936 and 1993. The average annual price change was +0.05%. Neither figure is very different from first-quarter results.

Also like the first quarter, the long-term trend is correlated with the budget presentation schedule. From 1936 to 1959, when most Budget Days were in April, the second-quarter record was dismal: six up, 17 down, one quarter unchanged and an average loss of -1.06% per year.

During the next three decades, the price trend strengthened. The 1960s saw an average annual increase of +0.39%. Prices rose eight times in the 1970s at an average rate of +1.92%, equal to 63 points on a 3300 FT-SE 100. The 1980s saw seven price rises and an average share price increase of +0.72% per year (*see Table 4.4*).

Table 4.4

PERCENTAGE PRICE CHANGE FOR MARCH SINCE 1980

	March 1–8	March 9–15	March 16–23	March 24–31
1980	-2.44%	-3.47%	-2.27%	-0.67%
1981	-3.45%	-2.43%	5.03%	5.37%
1982	3.07%	0.30%	-0.27%	0.74%
1983	4.22%	1.35%	-2.87%	0.12%
1984	2.18%	4.52%	1.82%	-1.63%
1985	0.71%	1.46%	-1.01%	-2.83%
1986	2.46%	3.97%	3.78%	-1.57%
1987	0.10%	-1.09%	1.74%	-2.13%
1988	1.97%	0.87%	-0.72%	-5.01%
1989	4.51%	1.73%	-3.19%	0.56%
1990	0.39%	-0.49%	1.72%	-1.53%
1991	2.51%	1.27%	-1.99%	0.51%
1992	-0.73%	-1.67%	-1.29%	0.21%
1993	3.85%	-1.03%	-1.39%	-0.57%
Average quarterly price change				
1980–89	1.33%	0.72%	0.21%	-0.71%
1980–93	1.38%	0.38%	-0.06%	-0.60%
Number of years in which prices:				
rose	11	8	5	6
fell	3	6	9	8

Table 4.4: The first and second quarters were extremely profitable in the 1980s. The third-quarter trend has been very weak since the 1987 crash. Prices have fallen in five of the past six years.

March 13th – look out

The daily price trend shows a similar pattern. The likelihood of a price rise on any day within the second quarter was decidedly lower in the 'old days' before March Budget Days became commonplace. Prices were especially likely to fall in the middle of the quarter, March 13th (*see Figure 4.6*).

In the *1994 Investor's Diary*, we reported on an interesting correlation between the first and second quarter that emerged in 1978. Since then, the first quarter rose by at least +0.71%

Figure 4.6

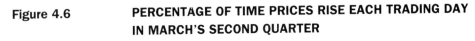

PERCENTAGE OF TIME PRICES RISE EACH TRADING DAY IN MARCH'S SECOND QUARTER

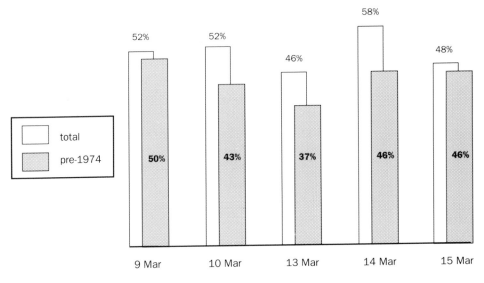

Figure 4.6: Prior to 1974, the price trend was noticeably weaker throughout the second quarter.

---

11 times and the second quarter followed 10 times. The single exception was in 1993 when the FT-SE 100 rose 89 points in the first quarter, an increase of over three percent, and the second quarter gave back some of that gain.

We suspect that Budget Day had a role in causing this relationship, and hypothesise that it will no longer be operative in the future.

But here is another relationship that has been in effect since 1936 and may still be operative. During this stretch, first-quarter prices fell by a small amount, -0.52% to -1.08% in nine years. Second-quarter prices continued to decline each time.

Rose (0) ▌

Fell (9) ▭

Second-quarter record after a price fall of -0.52% to -1.08% in the first quarter (since 1936)

THIRD QUARTER OF MARCH – MARCH 16TH TO 23RD

Unlike the first two quarters, whose recent record has improved, probably in response to Budget Day shifts, the record for pre-1970s third quarters looks better than the more recent one. Here again, Budget Day seems to play a role.

During the 1930s and 40s, a constant third-quarter investor would have made money by being fully invested during the third quarter of March. During the 1950s and '60s, prices rose in 13 years and fell six times (there was one no change year), one of the best records of the entire year in that period of time. Much of the profit was gained on March 21, which rose in most years. The other days of the quarter were profitable less than half the time (*see Figure 4.7*).

1970s' trend change

Things changed in the 1970s, the first losing decade on record. At first glance, the problem looks to be caused by the events of 1975. After an extraordinary rally during January and February of that year, the trend plateaued for the first two quarters of March and then dropped -11.47% in the third quarter, a temporary and long-overdue correction.

But the rest of the decade wasn't that good either. Although the remaining nine years showed an average annual third-quarter profit of +0.14%, the record was three up and six down.

The trend did strengthen in the Bull Market 1980s, but since the October 1987 crash, the record has been quite weak: one up and five down – tied with one other segment as the worst quarterly performer of the entire year – quite a change from the 1950s and '60s. In fact, over the last 20 years, from 1974 to 1993, the third-quarter record of seven up and 13 down is second worst (tied with three others) of the year.

Now that Budget Day has been shifted to November, we see a chance that the performance trend for March's third quarter will improve. However, we do not expect the improvement to rival the strength of the 1950s and '60s, as those years were aided by an approaching budget. We shall watch the situation carefully. For the moment, be careful.

Figure 4.7

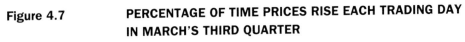

PERCENTAGE OF TIME PRICES RISE EACH TRADING DAY IN MARCH'S THIRD QUARTER

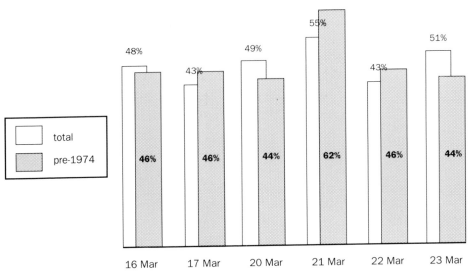

Figure 4.7: It is difficult to make money during the third quarter. Even in the good years of the 1940s to '60s, prices fell more often than they rose, the single exception being March 20.

FOURTH QUARTER OF MARCH – MARCH 24TH TO 31ST

The fourth quarter used to be a good time to hold shares. From 1940 to 1969, when the quarter was helped by a soon-to-arrive April budget, prices rose 67% of the time. The average annual increase in share prices was +0.62% and the price shifts on the last few days of the month were among the strongest of the entire month (*see Figure 4.8*).

Unfortunately, the trend began to change in the 1970s with a sub-average annual profit of +0.19%, and weakened still further during the 1980s. Prices fell six times including 1984, 1985, 1986 and 1987, the heart of the best Bull Market of the century. (In each of these four years, March as a whole was quite profitable.)

The last minute rush into PEPs has not helped share prices. Since their 1987 introduction, the record is three up and three down, with each up move relatively small and each down move

Figure 4.8

PERCENTAGE OF TIME PRICES RISE EACH TRADING DAY IN MARCH'S FOURTH QUARTER

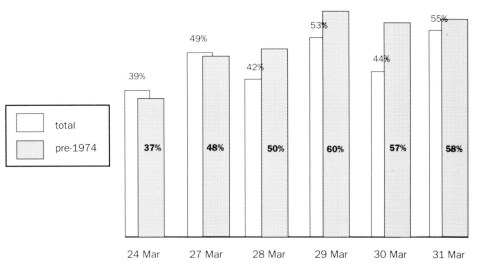

Figure 4.8: Prior to 1974, fourth-quarter prices frequently rose, especially during the last three days of the month. The trend was helped by the approach of Budget Day. But the profit trend then weakened as Budget Days were shifted to mid-March.

relatively large.

We forecast an improvement, now that spring budgets are gone, but not to the levels of the 1950s and 1960s which were aided by an approaching budget. Here is a statistical correlation that may help investors to predict profitable fourth quarters.

Watch third-quarter prices

Between 1936 and 1971, third-quarter prices shifted by a small amount 10 times, no more than -0.78% on the down-side and +0.56% on the up-side. Fourth-quarter prices rose all 10 times. Since the mid-1970s shift to a mid-March budget, this price signal stopped working. We shall wait to see if it comes alive again now that March budgets are a thing of the past.

Rose (10)

Fell (0)

Fourth-quarter record after a price shift of -0.78%to +0.56% in the third quarter (1936–71)

CHAPTER FIVE – APRIL 1995

> April has been consistently profitable for the past 50 years. Prices fell just six times from 1940–1989. Unfortunately, the party is probably over, a victim of the switch to a unified November budget, and the expectation of profit which, in the perverse world of investing, usually causes a loss.
>
> Be especially cautious during the first and third quarters of the month which have been quite weak in the past few years.

April is the year's second-best month over the long-run. A hypothetical £1,000 April investment in 1919 (moved into cash in the other 11 months) would have grown to £4,334 by 1993.

The last time April investors lost money was in the 1930s. Since then the month has been consistently profitable, a 50-year run. During this period, its worst performance was in the 1940s when it was fourth-best month and produced an average annual profit of +1.70%. In the four decades that followed, it was ranked either number one or two. Prices rose in eight or nine out of 10 years in the 1950s, '60s and '70s. In the 1980s prices rose all 10 years, a rare event that has occurred just one other time (January 1940 – 49). Is it any surprise that many investors think April is the closest thing to a one-way bet that the stock market offers? (*see Table 5.1*)

Unfortunately, the price trend has weakened in the 1990s. The record so far – two up and two down. Some investors may think it is too early to forecast a trend change. We are more pessimistic. In our opinion, the glorious April trend is a thing of the past. From now on, prices will behave like other, more normal months, some ups and some downs. We offer two reasons to support this conclusion: the shift to a late November unified Budget Day and investors' expectation of April profits.

Budget Day

The April success story is heavily influenced by the spring budget. This influence is especially apparent when each April price shift is correlated with its corresponding spring budget date. One important point before beginning this analysis. We have ignored some important market-moving issues like the political and economic unrest just after World War I, the great

Table 5.1

APRIL PRICE RISES AND DECLINES: 1919–1993

	Average April price change	Up	Down/ no change
1920–29	-0.50%	4	6
1930–39	-0.93%	5	5
1940–49	1.70%	8	2
1950–59	4.17%	9	1
1960–69	2.21%	8	2
1970–79	5.76%	9	1
1980–89	3.31%	10	–
1990–93	0.51%	2	2
Average April price change	2.11%	55	20

Table 5.1: Prior to the 1940s, April was just an average performer. The climate then noticeably improved. In the last five decades, April investments were highly profitable. Prices rose in at least eight out of every 10 years. The spring budget probably provided some of the stimulus. Unfortunately, the 1990s price trend, so far, is noticeably weaker and, to make matters worse, the spring budget has been shifted to November.

depression, uncertainties in the run-up to World War II, the painful recession of the early 1970s and the incredible Bull Market of the 1980s. Our focus is solely on the correlation between the date of Budget Day and April price shifts.

We also eliminated one monthly price shift from our analysis, the +25.69% increase of 1975, an extremely sharp up-move, and more a function of the recovery from the 1973–74 Bear Market. Doubters could argue we are loading the dice in our favour. Nevertheless, here goes.

In the 1920s and '30s, when 15 of 20 budgets were presented on April 16th or later, April's prices rose just half the time. It was seventh-ranked in the '20s and ninth-ranked in the '30s. Prices fell each year, on average, in both decades. In the 1940s to '80s, when most budgets were presented in March to mid-April, the April price trend considerably improved. Furthermore, as Figure 5.1 shows, the earlier that Budget Day arrived, the higher the profit.

Spring budgets are now a thing of the past. Where does this

Figure 5.1

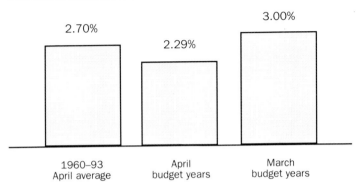

AVERAGE MONTHLY PERFORMANCE: 1960–1993

Figure 5.1: Profits were one-third higher in years following a March budget (1975 excluded).

---

leave April? No one knows for sure. But the historical evidence suggests that April's superb performance has been helped by the spring budget and that its future performance will now change.

When to buy

There are two useful investment principles which have consistently helped investors to out-perform the averages over the long-run: the Buy When It Hurts theory of picking market bottoms and the Don't Be A Pig theory of taking profits. The titles are tongue-in-cheek but each principle is deadly serious.

To Buy When It Hurts is to buy when the news is very bad. It is often time to buy when your stomach churns from the pain of your losses, when it is painful even to look at the stock market pages of your daily newspaper, when you swear to yourself 'Never again. The stock market is a fool's game' and when the biggest braggart you know has stopped telling you about his foolproof buy/sell system.

When to sell

The Don't Be A Pig follower knows that stock markets are dangerous and unpredictable. Like the losing general whose perfect strategy won the war, on paper, a pig forgets that surprises occur and markets don't always follow the script. According to one stock market wag:

Bulls make money sometimes

Bears make money sometimes

Pigs make money never

Baron Rothschild said it best when explaining how he made all his money: 'I always sell too soon'.

Success breeds failure

To this important list, may we add a third guiding principle: Success Breeds Failure. Stock markets simply cannot follow the same trend forever, even if an underlying stimulus continues to be in force. Human nature eventually forces the market's trend to change as investors become aware of a likely event, and try to take advantage of this knowledge. (If you thought you knew which way prices were likely to move tomorrow, wouldn't you act on that information?)

▶ Perhaps money is committed to the market earlier, thereby reducing the concentrated flow which drove up prices in the first place.

▶ Perhaps money leaves the market a bit earlier, knowing a weak stretch is likely to occur soon, thereby removing the concentrated selling pressure that formerly drove down prices or causing the decline to happen a little earlier.

For these reasons, we do not expect the April price trend to remain as strong as it was in the past. We do not know if its new pattern will be more like the horrors of May and June or the more neutral pattern of February. Either way, we expect April's prices to fall more often than they did in the past.

Forecasting tips

In view of the uncertainty surrounding April, historic price trends that forecast which way April prices are most likely to move are especially valuable. Here are several trends which have done a good job in the past of anticipating April price shifts. Each has been in effect for many decades, and is based on price shifts over the past several months or the past year, not on what just happened in March (which could be budget-related).[1]

One useful trend is the direction of prices in the past 12 months, April 1st to March 31st. A sharp up-move often tips rising April prices. Since 1923, there have been 20 years when

---

[1] Reminder: All monthly calculations are based on the FT-Non Financial Index, formerly the FT-'500'; unless otherwise stated, they are based on data from 1919–1993. All daily, quarterly, and bi-monthly calculations are based on the Ordinary Share Index, also known as the FT-30; unless otherwise stated, they are based on data from 1936–1993.

12-month trend

prices rose in the preceding 12 months by +19.26% or more. April share prices rose 19 times. The single exception was back in 1960.

Rose (19)

Fell (1)

April record after a price rise of at least +19.26% in past 12 months (since 1923)

Another trend associated with rising April prices is a decline in the last 12 months of -4.93% to -12.53%. Since 1948, in 14 years with a price decline within this range, April prices rose every time.

Rose (14)

Fell (0)

April record after a price fall of -4.93% to -12.53% in past 12 months (since 1948)

First-quarter trend

A third trend to watch is the direction of prices in the year's first quarter. Since 1922, prices rose in this three month period by at least +4.38% on 29 separate occasions. April's prices rose in 27 of those years (93%).

Rose (27)

Fell (2)

April record after a price rise of at least +4.38% in past three months (since 1922)

Are these three trends still operative in April's new trading environment? Only time will tell.

FIRST QUARTER OF APRIL – APRIL 1ST TO 8TH

Over the years, each quarter of April has been quite profitable (*see Table 5.2*). The best performer of all was the first quarter. Prices rose 64% of the time during this quarter, generating an average annual profit of +0.80%, one of the six best quarterly performances for the entire year. First-quarter share prices increased in value in every single decade on record, with the best trading days of the quarter being April 3rd to April 5th, the end of the tax year (*see Figure 5.2*). It was either the most profitable or second most profitable segment of the month from the 1930s to the 1970s.

Table 5.2

PERCENT PRICE CHANGE: APRIL 1936–1993

	April 1–8	April 9–15	April 16–23	April 24–30
Average annual price change				
1936–39	1.59%	-0.34%	-0.26%	-1.01%
1940–49	0.54%	0.04%	0.38%	0.56%
1950–59	1.96%	1.20%	0.88%	-0.45%
1960–69	0.67%	0.28%	0.63%	0.79%
1970–79	1.08%	0.76%	1.96%	0.80%
1980–89	0.13%	0.62%	0.76%	2.18%
1990–93	-0.97%	3.03%	-0.90%	-0.57%
Average quarterly price change	0.80%	0.68%	0.71%	0.56%
Number of years in which prices:				
rose	37	36	35	38
fell	20	20	22	20
remained unchanged	1	2	1	–

Table 5.2: Each of April's four quarters has been quite profitable over the long-run. Strongest of all was the first quarter, consistently either best or second-best performer of the month. But the first-quarter and third-quarter trends have noticeably weakened since 1980, around the time Budget Day was moved to March. The second quarter continues to be strong, perhaps due to its role as the opening quarter of the new tax year.

Figure 5.2

PERCENTAGE OF TIME PRICES RISE EACH TRADING DAY IN APRIL'S FIRST QUARTER

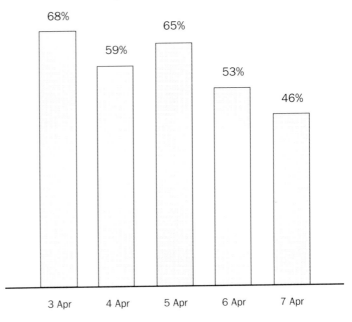

Figure 5.2: Over the long-term, the first few trading days of the quarter (end of the tax year) are the most profitable. If you plan to purchase any shares, the odds favour completing your transaction at the very beginning of the quarter.

Unfortunately, the trend has changed recently. During the 1980s, in the midst of a fabulously profitable Bull Market, first-quarter prices rose just three times. The trend changed around the time that spring budgets were moved up to mid-March. Many of the losses were small so the decade still showed an average annual gain – of just +0.13%. The 1990s record? More of the same with one up and three down.

Year's worst

To put things into perspective, in the last 10 years, 1984 to 1993, first-quarter prices have risen just twice, the very worst performance of the year (*see Table 5.3*). It is quite rare for such a drastic trend change to occur, causing the same segment of the month to be on a 'Best' list and 'Worst' list at the same time.

The 1987 introduction of PEPs has not helped this final quarter of the year. The common assumption is that lots of PEP money pours into shares at the very last minute to beat the end-

Table 5.3: **YEAR'S SIX BEST AND SIX WORST QUARTERS IN LAST 10 YEARS: 1984–1993**

Best	Number of increases	Worst	Number of increases
January 4th quarter	9	April 1st quarter	2
March 1st quarter	9	March 4th quarter	3
January 3rd quarter	8	April 3rd quarter	3
February 3rd quarter	8	June 4th quarter	3
April 2nd quarter	8	July 3rd quarter	3
August 4th quarter	8	October 4th quarter	3

Table 5.3: It's hard to believe but it's true. One of the best months in history has two entries on a list of the year's six worst quarters. The first and third quarters have become points in the year in which it is best to stand aside.

of-year tax deadline, driving up share prices. The theory is not supported by the facts. Since their introduction, first-quarter prices have fallen in four out of six years.

What's ahead for this quarter?

Will the move from a mid-March budget allow prices to regain their former profitability? Or has the shift to November added additional down-side pressure to the price trend? Only time will tell.

For the present, investors should be very cautious during this part of the month. Assuming prices continue their pattern of recent weakness, why jump in at the beginning of the month if you can buy at a better price by waiting a few days? And sadly, the budget date switch undermines each historical trend that once helped to forecast the direction of first-quarter share price shifts. We think the best strategy is to stand aside.

A possible exception

For readers who disagree and think the patterns of the past will continue, or who think unique trading conditions will make this year an exception to the rule, here is a trend that possibly could help. Between 1936 and 1993, there were 28 years when prices shifted by a small margin of -1.35% to +0.72% in March's fourth quarter. April first-quarter prices rose in 24 of those years (86%). Each exception occurred after the introduction of mid-March budgets.

Table 5.4   **APRIL FIRST QUARTER/MARCH FOURTH QUARTER CORRELATION**

	Up	Down	Typical date of budget
1936–39	3	-	late April
1940–49	7	-	various points in April
1950–59	5	-	mid April
1960–69	3	-	mid April
1970–79	4	-	late March and early April
1980–89	1	2	mid March
1990–93	1	2	mid March
Total	24	4	

Table 5.4: Direction of April first-quarter prices after March fourth-quarter price shift of -1.35% to +0.72%

If first-quarter price ebbs and flows follow past patterns, now that March budgets have been eliminated, this trend could be useful. We admit to being dubious!

SECOND QUARTER OF APRIL – APRIL 9TH TO APRIL 15TH

Shares rose 62% of the time in the year's opening fiscal quarter between 1936 and 1993. Prices increased by +0.68% per year, on average. Unlike the first quarter, the recent trend remains strong. The average annual increase in the 1970s was +0.76% (six out of 10 years increased, one no change). The average annual increase for the 1980s was +0.62% (seven out of 10 years increased) (*see Table 5.5*).

One of the best quarters

The record since the 1987 crash is six out of six increases for the first full quarter of the new year, tied with one other quarter as the year's best during this recent stretch of time. We are intrigued by this strong performance given the weakness of the adjacent first and third quarters during the same period of time. Each is, recently, among the year's very worst performers. A possible explanation: the start of a new tax year releases a short-lived flood of new money, providing a brief boost to prices.

Analysis of trading conditions on a day-by-day basis finds

Table 5.5

PERCENTAGE PRICE CHANGE FOR APRIL SINCE 1980

	April 1–8	April 9–15	April 16–23	April 24–30
1980	-0.07%	2.60%	-0.59%	1.19%
1981	2.14%	1.80%	6.41%	2.22%
1982	-1.44%	-2.77%	4.09%	1.41%
1983	3.04%	3.04%	-1.08%	1.06%
1984	-1.32%	3.44%	-1.70%	3.42%
1985	-0.19%	1.51%	-1.78%	1.23%
1986	-0.14%	-1.25%	-0.64%	2.42%
1987	-1.17%	-2.79%	2.65%	3.65%
1988	1.93%	0.16%	-0.29%	2.29%
1989	-1.46%	0.48%	0.56%	2.93%
1990	-1.61%	0.05%	-2.77%	-2.31%
1991	2.31%	0.23%	-1.89%	-0.62%
1992	-2.56%	10.69%	-0.50%	1.50%
1993	-2.01%	1.15%	1.57%	-0.85%
Average quarterly price change				
1980–89	0.13%	0.62%	0.76%	2.18%
1980–93	-0.18%	1.31%	0.29%	1.40%
Number of years in which prices:				
rose	4	11	5	11
fell	10	3	9	3

Table 5.5: Since 1980, first- and third-quarter prices have fallen in most years. The second quarter (the fiscal year's opening quarter) and the fourth quarter continue to be profitable. Prices have been especially strong in the second quarter since the 1987 crash, with a record of six up and none down.

---

that prices are relatively weak in the middle of the quarter. April 12th rises just 40% of the time. But this weakness is largely due to its performance in the 1930s to '60s. In the last 20 years, April 12th has performed as strongly as the other days of the period – profitable in most years (*see Figure 5.3*).

On balance, if you are thinking of selling shares during this quarter, the odds favour holding on until its end. However, a newly-developing price trend may be of interest to readers who

Figure 5.3

PERCENTAGE OF TIME PRICES RISE EACH TRADING DAY IN APRIL'S SECOND QUARTER

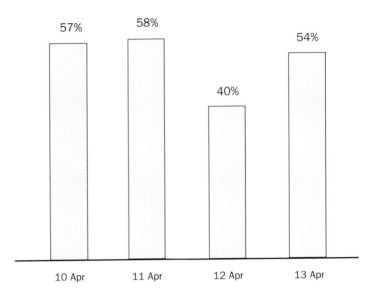

Figure 5.3: Most second-quarter trading days tend to be profitable. The record of the single loser, April 12th, has improved in the past 20 years. Its recent record is comparable to the other days in this quarter.

A new trend?

who wish to make a second-quarter transaction.

Since 1980, every second-quarter loss has been tipped by a small price drop of -0.14% to -1.44% in the first quarter. All other second quarters have been profitable.

Correlation between price shifts in April's first and second quarters

	Second quarter	
First-quarter shift	Up	Down
-0.13% or better	5	–
-0.14% to -1.44%	2	3
-1.45% or worse	4	–

The data suggest that a small decline in the last quarter of the year is a stimulus for more of the same as the new year begins. But if bigger losses are incurred in the year's final quarter, perhaps triggered by tax-related considerations, the decks are cleared for a good start to the new year. On the up-side, investors who sense good trading conditions around the start of the new year tip their hand in the last week of the old year.

Important reminder

This trend is based on a period of just 14 years. Treat it as a hypothesis, not a confirmed relationship. Likewise, our description of the underlying cause are guesses, not informed statements of fact.

Despite the favourable trading conditions, it is not a particularly good point at which to commit new funds because of the high probability of a third-quarter price drop.

THIRD QUARTER OF APRIL – APRIL 16TH TO APRIL 23RD

Like April's first quarter, the third quarter was traditionally quite good to investors, producing an average yearly profit in every decade on record. Between 1936 and 1993, third-quarter prices rose 60% of the time. The average annual profit was +0.71%. Trading conditions were good throughout the quarter with the likelihood of a price rise peaking on April 19th when prices rise 67% of the time (*see Figure 5.4*).

Also like the first quarter, things may be changing for the worse. The 1980s price trend was a warning signal. The beginning of the decade produced all of this quarter's profits (1981, +6.41%; 1982, +4.09%). Even though a strong Bull Market dominated the decade, and the full month consistently generated high profits, prices rose in only two of the decade's remaining eight years. Note that the March budget was presented at least four weeks earlier during this period, reducing the odds that short-term budget effects were exerting pressure on third-quarter prices.

Poor recent trend

In the last 10 years, third-quarter prices have risen just three times, one of the worst performances of the entire year. Unfortunately, with a good probability of a fourth-quarter profit, investors have no incentive to sell shares at the beginning of this quarter. By the same token, there is no incentive to commit additional money either.

We are distrustful of most historical trends that forecast

Figure 5.4   **PERCENTAGE OF TIME PRICES RISE EACH TRADING DAY IN APRIL'S THIRD QUARTER**

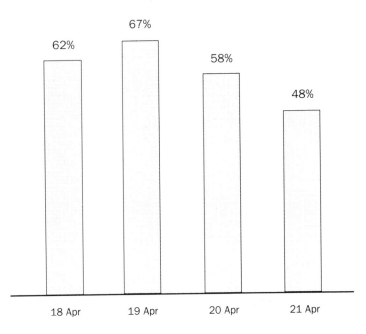

Figure 5.4: Trading conditions used to be quite good throughout the quarter. Unfortunately, in the recent past the trend has weakened across the board

Watch the second quarter

third-quarter price shifts because of the possible influence of the spring budget. But two relationships may still be worth watching. One involves the second-quarter price trend. If prices decline, they often rise in the third quarter. Since 1942, there have been 15 occasions when share prices declined in the second quarter. The third quarter bounced back with an increase in 13 of them (87%). Shares gained +1.73% on average during these 15 years. During this period, Budget Day advanced from late April, through early April to mid-March, suggesting the trend is not (just) Budget Day-related. The signal last flashed in 1987 when Budget Day was on March 17th. April's second-quarter fall of -2.79% was followed with a +2.65% increase in the third quarter.

Rose (13)

Fell (2)

Third-quarter record after a second-quarter price decline (since 1942)

Another signal, very new, seems to be rearing its head. Since 1976, a rise of at least +1.32% in April's first half has been associated with a decline in the third quarter in nine out of 10 occurrences. As with other trends that appear during this part of the year, we are unsure of the effect of Budget Day and shall watch the situation carefully.

Rose (1)

Fell (9)

Third-quarter record after a first half price rise of at least +1.32% (since 1976)

FOURTH QUARTER OF APRIL – APRIL 24TH TO APRIL 30TH

Prices rise 66% of the time during the fourth quarter of April, the third-best quarter of the year. Between 1936 and 1993, the average annual increase in share prices was +0.56%. April 27th is especially good to investors. Prices rise three out of four times on this day, one of the year's best performances (*see Figure 5.5*).

The only full decade in which the fourth segment of the month failed to produce a profit was in the 1950s when it dropped at a rate of -0.45% per year.

No recent weakness

Unlike the first and third quarters of the month, no sign of weakness has been detected in the fourth quarter during the 1980s. Prices rose in all 10 years at a superb average annual rate of +2.18%, the best level of profit for any quarter in April since records began.

Here's a statistical relationship to help investors pin-point profitable fourth quarters. If prices rise in the third quarter, the

Figure 5.5

PERCENTAGE OF TIME PRICES RISE EACH TRADING DAY IN APRIL'S FOURTH QUARTER

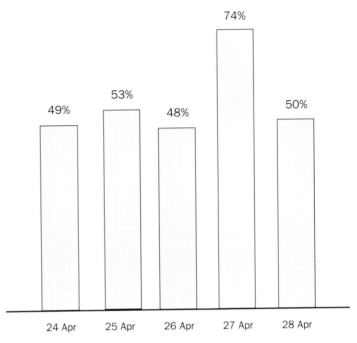

Figure 5.5: The strength of April 27 continues right up to the present. Prices have risen on 11 of the last 14 April 27ths.

odds are high that fourth-quarter prices will also rise. The trend has been quite hot since 1959. The shift to a mid-March budget had not affected this price signal. Here is the evidence: since 1959, there were 18 years when the third quarter rose up to 6.41%. The fourth quarter rose in 16 of them (89%), with an average gain of +1.78%.

Rose (16)

Fell (2)

Fourth-quarter record after a third quarter price rise of up to 6.41% (since 1959)

Chapter Six – May 1995

> May is the eleventh-best investment month. Shares fall -0.46% on average. Most analysts conclude it's a bad time to own shares. They are wrong. Don't be too quick to 'Sell in May and go away'. The real problem in May are Big Hits – declines of at least 5% which occur every five or six years. If you can avoid Big Hit years, you will make money with a May investment. Fortunately, the price trend in the run-up to May often tips off when a Big Hit is likely.
>
> Keep in mind that the first quarter is usually profitable, regardless of what is in store in the rest of the month

According to conventional wisdom, May is a poor month in which to hold shares – and has been for three-quarters of this century.

At first glance, the argument against a May investment in shares is quite persuasive. May investors have lost money in every single decade on record except for the 1950s. From 1919 to 1993, prices fell at a yearly average of -0.46%, equal to 15 points on a 3300 FT-SE 100 (*see Table 6.1*). Only June produces poorer results. A May investor who started with £1,000 in 1919, shifting into cash for the other 11 months of the year, would now be worth just £646. Is there any wonder that conventional wisdom advises investors to 'Sell in May and go away. Don't come back 'til St Leger's Day'?

But don't listen. Conventional wisdom is wrong. Consider these six facts:

First quarter is profitable

May losses usually occur in the second to the fourth segments of the month. The first quarter tends to be profitable. Prices rise 60% of the time. The average annual profit is +0.41%. That's equal to 14 points on a 3300 FT-SE 100 (*see Figure 6.1*). It's a perfectly safe time in which to own shares. Yes, you will lose money in some years but over the long run, the profits will outweigh the losses by a wide margin. So even if the May-bashers are right, don't move out of shares on May 1st.

Table 6.1 | **MAY PRICE RISES AND DECLINES: 1919–1993**

	Average May price change	Up	Down/ no change
1920–29	-0.73%	5	5
1930–39	-1.45%	3	7
1940–49	-0.63%	7	3
1950–59	0.52%	6	4
1960–69	-1.35%	3	7
1970–79	-1.37%	5	5
1980–89	-0.88%	4	6
1990–93	3.43%	4	–
Average May price change	-0.46%	38	37

Table 6.1: The price of the average share has fallen in every decade but one since the 1920s. Big Hits of -5% or worse are the source of May's problems. Prices usually fall by a large amount once or twice a decade. The rest of the decade tends to be quite profitable. If you can avoid the Big Hits, a May investment can be quite profitable over the long-run.

Foreign factors count

We live in a global economy. Narrow national interests are increasingly undermined by international forces. This is especially true in the stock market. Organisations like the European Community and GATT have a large and rapidly growing effect on the profits of our local businesses. The competence or lack of by foreign governments in America, Japan, Germany, etc, plays a huge role in our local economy. Witness the wild gyration in share prices here when tanks opened fire on the Kremlin or whenever the Chairman of the Federal Reserve makes a comment about the American economy. Foreign funds account for a constantly growing share of UK investment capital. Decisions by these foreign investors to buy or sell are often stimulated by conditions at the source of their funds – their local market, not ours.

Speculators would change the trend

Multi-billion pound hedge funds, specifically set up to exploit short-term speculative opportunities, jump in and out of the world's stock markets at the flick of a computer button. Assuming May prices did drop with sufficient predictability to

Figure 6.1

PROFITABILITY OF MAY'S FOUR QUARTERS

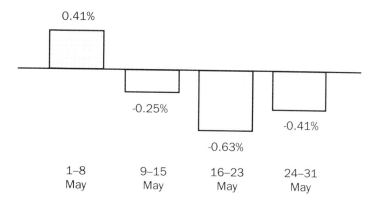

Figure 6.1: The first quarter is profitable in most years. The trend soon deteriorates. The third-quarter price trend is a horror. Prices drop 62% of the time, the year's worst quarterly performance. The size of the average annual price drop is -0.63%, equal to 21 points on a 3300 FT-SE 100.

interest these investors, the weight of money would quickly change the underlying trend. For example: If 'smart money' knew May prices would drop, they would sell short or purchase Puts at the end of April to catch the May drop. Prices would then fall in late April because of this selling pressure (whereas, at present, late April prices usually don't fall) and rise in May in the absence of heavy selling, or as speculators rush to cover their short positions.

November Budget Day

History tells us that Budget Days are usually good for investors. Let us assume, for the sake of discussion, that some past spring budget rallies were followed by a partial retraction against the up-turn in May. If so, the switch from a March/April budget to a late November date eliminates this source of May weakness.

Big Hits are the problem

Despite the published claims, May is profitable in most years. May share prices rise 51% of the time. The real problem in May: share prices take a very bad 'hit' every few years, large enough to affect the average performance for the whole decade. There have been 14 years with price declines of 5% or more.[1] They seem to occur once every five or six years. On this dimension, May has the dubious distinction of being ranked joint Number One, with June.

Here's how the May investor fared since 1920. Money was lost in the 1920s due to an -11.21% price drop in 1920. Prices rose in five of the decade's other nine years. There was a -9.03% drop in 1931 and -7.53% drop in 1932 which hurt the 1930s average. The 1940s was another loser, due to just one drop of -11.60% in 1940. Prices rose in the rest of the decade by an average of +0.59% per year (seven up, two down).

The market fell -8.69% in 1952. The rest of the decade rose at an average yearly rate of +1.54%. The 1960s average annual loss of -1.35% would have been more than halved to -0.52% had it not been for an -8.82% decline in 1962.

The 1970s witnessed two large declines, -7.14% in 1970 and -8.08% in 1974. As a result, the decade was a losing proposition for investors. The 1980s was affected by a -10.53% decline in 1984. The price of the average share rose in the rest of the decade.

Recent record is strong

If you are still not convinced that ' Sell in May' is bad advice, consider this: May's record since 1989 is six consecutive up-moves. This is the first time since records began in 1919 that May prices rose six times in a row. It doesn't mean that prices will always rise in May. But it certainly contradicts the theory that May is a loser to be consistently avoided.

Avoid Big Hit years

The key issue to address in this difficult investment month is how to avoid the occasional profit-wrecking Big Hits. If there were a way of avoiding Big Hit years, May investors would profit handsomely. They would still encounter some losing years but the winners would more than compensate for those 'normal' sized losers. Is there such a way? In a word, yes.

---

[1] Reminder: All monthly calculations are based on the FT-Non-Financial Index, formerly the FT-'500'; unless otherwise stated, they are based on data from 1919–1993. All daily, quarterly, and bi-monthly calculations are based on the Ordinary Share Index, also known as the FT-30; unless otherwise stated, they are based on data from 1936–1993.

The best way to avoid Big Hit years is to monitor the size of the April price change. If April prices shift by a small amount, declining by less than -1.66% or rising by no more than +2.83%, there is a low likelihood of a Big Hit in May. There have been 34 years in which April prices either rose or fell within this range. There were no 5% plus May price declines in any of these years (*see Figure 6.2*).

Another way to avoid Big Hits is to watch the price trend in the preceding 12 months. May prices never declined by 5% or more if prices in the past 12 months moved within a range of -1.63% to +15.34%. There have been 23 years in which prices either rose or fell within this range. There were no 5% plus May price declines in any of these years. Obviously, important fresh economic or political news could throw May prices into a tailspin, regardless of what either historical trend suggests, but the odds of this happening are low unless the news catches the markets by surprise.

Eliminating duplication between these two trends, there were 46 years when prices in the past month or past 12 months moved within the designated ranges. No Big Hit occurred in any of these years. In the remaining 29 years on record, a Big Hit occurred 14 times – almost a 50% 'success' rate.

Figure 6.2

PERCENTAGE OF TIME PRICES FALL BY 5% OR MORE IN MAY

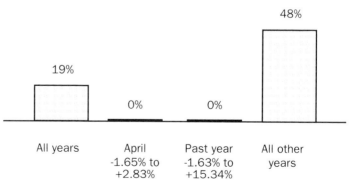

Figure 6.2: Big Hits occur every five or six years on average. None has occurred since 1984. They usually don't occur in years with small price fluctuations in the previous month, or in the past 12 months. But in an 'all other' year – look out. There were 14 Big Hits in 29 'all other' years.

Aside from avoiding Big Hit years, you can also increase profits by identifying specific years when May prices are especially likely to rise. Short sellers or Put buyers can also profit by identifying years with a high likelihood of May price drops. Here are two trends which, historically, have done a good job of anticipating the direction of May price shifts.

There have been 15 years in which share prices satisfied two conditions: *(a)* they rose in March and April by at least +1.33% in total, and *(b)* they rose in April within a range of +0.70% to +2.81%. May prices rose each time.

Rose (15)

Fell (0)

May record after a March/April price rise of at least +1.33% and an April rise of +0.70% to +2.81%

On the other hand if prices rise too high in April, May prices often suffer. There have been nine years when April's prices increased between +5.59% to +8.31%. The May record in those years is zero up and nine down.

Rose (0)

Fell (9)

May record after an April price rise of +5.59% to +8.31%

First Quarter of May – May 1st to May 8th

Although May can be a poor investment month, the first quarter is a consistent money-maker. A first-quarter investment in each year on record since 1936 produced an average annual profit of +0.41%. Presumably the final phase of April's rally spills over to this segment of May.

In contrast, the rest of the month typically produces an average loss: second quarter, -0.25%; third quarter, -0.63%; fourth quarter, -0.41% (*see Table 6.2*).

Table 6.2

PERCENTAGE PRICE CHANGE: MAY 1936–1993

	May 1–8	May 9–15	May 16–23	May 24–31
Average annual price change				
1936–39	1.51%	-1.08%	-1.11%	-0.24%
1940–49	0.46%	0.00%	-0.84%	-0.64%
1950–59	0.75%	-0.23%	0.14%	0.61%
1960–69	-0.35%	-0.04%	-1.35%	-0.59%
1970–79	0.64%	-0.35%	-0.46%	-1.84%
1980–89	-0.39%	-0.28%	-1.26%	-0.06%
1990–93	1.62%	-0.33%	1.46%	0.56%
Average quarterly price change	0.41%	-0.25%	-0.63%	-0.41%
Number of years in which prices:				
rose	35	32	23	28
fell	23	26	35	30

Table 6.2: The first-quarter investor often profits. But the second-quarter investor loses money in the long-run despite the fact that prices rise in most second quarters. The declines in down years are bigger than the profits in up years. The third quarter is a long-term money-loser, the worst or next-to-worst quarter of the month in every decade through the 1980s. The fourth quarter also tends to be a loser although the direction of prices in the run-up to it often provides good clues to its profitability.

Prices are usually strong at the very beginning of the month. They rise on May 2, 3, and 4 in six out of 10 years and are the best trading days of the entire month. If you are planning to sell shares at this point of the year, waiting until May 4th will be a profit-maker more often than a profit-loser (*see Figure 6.3*).

The odds of a first-quarter profit can be improved by watching for a small price shift during April. If prices move within a range of -1.29% to +2.81%, the odds of a first-quarter profit are high. Since 1936, there were 22 April shifts within this range. First-quarter prices rose 19 times (86%), at an average annual rate of +1.03%.

Rose (19)

Fell (3)

First-quarter record after an April price shift of -1.29% to +2.81%

In the *1994 Investor's Diary*, we pointed out a relationship between the direction of price movements during April's third and fourth quarters, and this quarter of May. If prices rose in both April quarters, they often continue to rise in the beginning of May. Here is an update on that relationship which heightens the odds of a profit. If prices rise in both April quarters, with a third-quarter rise under 6% and a fourth-quarter rise no higher than +2.65%, the odds are high that prices will continue to rise in the first quarter. Out of 24 years with price increases of the required size in April, they continued to rise in the first quarter of May 20 times (83%) and generated an average annual profit of +1.00%.

Figure 6.3

PERCENTAGE OF TIME PRICES RISE EACH TRADING DAY IN MAY'S FIRST QUARTER

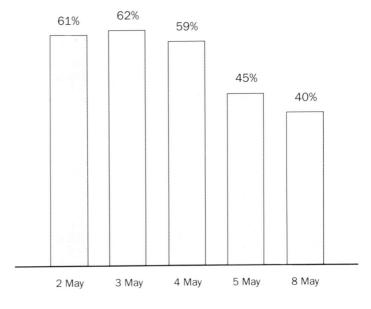

Figure 6.3: May 2–4 are the best three trading days of the month. In most years, it would pay not to sell any shares until May 4.

Rose (19)

Fell (4)

First-quarter record after a price rise in April's third quarter
(under 6%) and fourth quarter (no more than +2.65%)

Although prices often rise during the first quarter, they do decline on occasion. A decline of any size in April's third quarter, or a tiny rise (no more than +0.20%), followed by an increase in the fourth quarter, or a tiny fall (no more than -0.04%), often tips off that prices will drop in May's first quarter. Since 1947, there were 12 years when prices declined in the third quarter of April (or rose very slightly) and rose in the fourth quarter (or declined very slightly). May first-quarter prices fell in 10 of them (83%).

Rose (2)

Fell (10)

First-quarter record after a third-quarter shift of +0.20% or lower
and fourth-quarter shift of -0.04% or higher (since 1947)

SECOND QUARTER OF MAY – MAY 9TH TO MAY 15TH

The second quarter of May has cost investors money in every decade on record except for the 1940s when prices broke exactly even. Daily share price trends tend to be disappointing throughout the entire quarter. Prices tend to fall more often than they rise except for the 15th of the month (*see Figure 6.4*). The trend did not even improve during the 1980s' Bull Market decade when prices rose just five times and generated an average annual loss of -0.28%.

Prices continue to disappoint – so bet against the market

Prices continue to disappoint right up to the present. The record since the 1987 crash is three up and three down with a small average loss of -0.12% (*see Table 6.3*).

87

Figure 6.4

PERCENTAGE OF TIME PRICES RISE EACH TRADING DAY IN MAY'S SECOND QUARTER

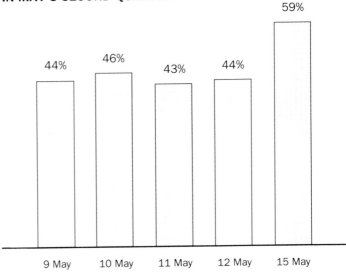

Figure 6.4: Prices frequently drop throughout the quarter. The odds favour standing aside during this segment of the month unless a unique situation arises.

The best way to profit in this quarter of May is to bet against the market. In the *1994 Investor's Diary*, we advised readers to watch the direction of first-quarter prices. If they fall, there is a 68% chance they will continue to fall in the second quarter. Here's an update on that price signal that will increase the odds of making a profit.

There have been 14 occasions since 1936 when April's prices rose in a range of +2.83% to +8.31%, and were followed by a fall in May's first quarter. Second-quarter prices continued to decline in 11 of those years (79%). The average second-quarter decline during those 14 years was -1.31%, equal to 43 points on an FT-SE 100 in the area of 3300.

Rose (3)

Fell (11)

Second-quarter record after an April price rise of +2.83% to +8.31% and a fall in May's first quarter

Table 6.3

PERCENTAGE PRICE CHANGE FOR MAY SINCE 1980

	May 1–8	May 9–15	May 16–23	May 24–31
1980	-0.84%	0.25%	-3.31%	-1.75%
1981	-4.69%	-1.46%	-3.14%	-0.17%
1982	1.43%	1.25%	-5.08%	4.76%
1983	-0.13%	-3.27%	3.08%	2.90%
1984	-0.58%	-2.96%	-3.46%	-5.98%
1985	1.76%	3.42%	-1.18%	-0.76%
1986	-4.16%	-2.57%	2.21%	-0.77%
1987	2.90%	1.98%	-0.29%	1.51%
1988	-0.26%	-0.80%	-1.47%	1.41%
1989	0.70%	1.39%	0.01%	-1.77%
1990	3.42%	1.26%	4.53%	2.49%
1991	1.56%	-2.92%	1.00%	0.61%
1992	2.96%	-1.00%	1.72%	-1.66%
1993	-1.44%	1.32%	-1.40%	0.80%
Average quarterly price change				
1980–89	-0.39%	-0.28%	-1.26%	-0.06%
1980–93	0.19%	-0.29%	-0.48%	0.12%
Number of years in which prices:				
rose	7	7	6	7
fell	7	7	8	7

Table 6.3: May timing signals worked well in the 1980s. In 1980, '81, '83, '84, and '88, an April price rise of +2.83% to +8.31%, followed by a first-quarter decline signalled a second-quarter fall four out of five times. There were two occasions when second and third-quarter prices fell, with the second-quarter fall in a range of -0.86% to -4.32%. Fourth-quarter prices followed. One positive note: third-quarter prices rose four times in a row, 1989–92, the first time ever. Is the trend changing? We will watch carefully.

Just as a rising April trend, followed by a price decline in May's first-quarter signals that second-quarter prices are likely to fall, rising April prices followed by a price rise in the first quarter of May is a signal that second-quarter prices will rise. There have been 21 years when April prices rose by no more than +5.48% and first-quarter prices rose by +0.62% to +4.00%. Second-quarter prices continued to rise in 18 of those years (86%). The average increase was +0.93%.

Rose (18)

Fell (3)

Second-quarter record after an April price rise of up to +5.48% and a rise in May's first quarter of +0.62% to +4.00%

Third Quarter of May – May 16th to 23rd

Investors lost money by investing during the third quarter during the 1930s, '40s, '60s, '70s, and '80s. The only time a profit was made, and a small one at that, was back in the 1950s.

Between 1936 and 1993, the third quarter of May rose just 40% of the time, the worst performance of any quarter of the year, and generated an average loss of -0.63%, second-worst of the year. Even during the 1980s, prices fell seven times. The only way to profit consistently in this quarter is to bet on falling prices.

There are no pockets of strength during the quarter. Analysis of daily price trends finds two trading days that manage to rise 50% of the time. The rest fall in most years (*see Figure 6.5*).

Trends may be changing – but exercise caution

From 1989 to 1992, prices increased four consecutive years, for the first time ever. The previous best was three ups in a row back in 1958–1960. The up-trend record was broken in 1993 with a -1.40% decline in share prices. Still, the four year up-turn could be a preliminary signal that the third-quarter trend is in the process of change. On the other hand, it may simply be a random event. We don't know yet but we shall continue to watch carefully. For the moment, use extreme caution. Although investors might make a profit by holding shares in any single year, the odds strongly favour standing on the side-lines or betting against the market.

If you plan to bet on the down-side, maximise your gain by

Figure 6.5

PERCENTAGE OF TIME PRICES RISE EACH TRADING DAY IN MAY'S THIRD QUARTER

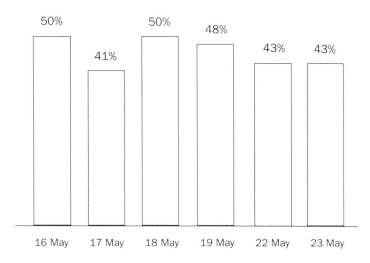

Figure 6.5: Another poor segment of the month. In most years, it makes sense to stand aside.

monitoring first- and second-quarter prices. If prices fall in the first quarter or rise a little bit (no more than +0.94%), and they fall in the second quarter, the odds of a third-quarter decline increase. Since 1936, there have been 19 occasions with first- and second-quarter price trends within the designated limits. In 16 of these years (84%), prices continued to decline in the third quarter. The average third-quarter loss was 1.76%, equal to 58 points on a 3300 FT-SE 100.

Rose (3)

Fell (16)

Third-quarter record after a first-quarter price shift of +0.94% or less and a second-quarter fall

FOURTH QUARTER OF MAY – MAY 24TH TO MAY 31ST

In some respects, the fourth quarter of May is a re-run of the third quarter. Investors consistently lose money by investing during the fourth quarter. The only decade on record in which profits were made was the 1950s.

Between 1936 and 1993, the fourth quarter of May rose 48% of the time and generated an average loss of -0.41%, tied with the second quarter of September as the fifth-worst record of the year. Analysis of daily price trends shows a steady pattern of declines. May 26th is especially poor with a 38% chance of rising, the month's worst performer (*see Figure 6.6*).

Maximise gains

But unlike the third quarter, smart investors can profit on the up-side as well as the down-side. Maximise gains by monitoring third-quarter prices.

In the *1994 Investor's Diary*, we pointed out that the odds of a fourth-quarter decline increase if share prices fall in the third quarter. Here's an update. If third-quarter prices fall by -3.10% to -5.50%, there is an 82% chance that prices will decline in the fourth quarter.

An even stronger down-side indicator is the trend in the second *and* third quarters of May. If the price of an average share falls in both quarters, with the second-quarter fall in a range of -0.86% to -4.32%, fourth-quarter prices will probably fall. Since 1938, out of nine moves within this range, fourth-quarter prices fell every time.

Rose (0)

Fell (9)

Fourth-quarter record after a second-quarter fall of -0.86% to -4.32% and a third-quarter fall (since 1938)

It's also possible to profit on the up-side during this segment of May. Watch for a steady up-trend in the first three quarters of the month. There have been 11 years since 1936 when prices rose in the first, second and third quarters of the month. Fourth-quarter prices rose in nine of those years.

Figure 6.6

PERCENTAGE OF TIME PRICES RISE EACH TRADING DAY IN MAY'S FOURTH QUARTER

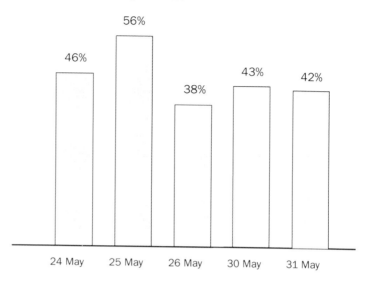

Figure 6.6: Another losing stretch in the long-run. May 25 is the best day of the quarter. But it is the only winning day. And it is followed by May 26, the worst day of the entire month.

Rose (9)

Fell (2)

Fourth-quarter record after a rise in the first, second, and third quarters

The two exceptions to the rule are instructive. In 1989, prices rose in the third quarter by just +0.01%, thereby qualifying by a whisker. Clearly, a real third-quarter rise is needed to push fourth-quarter prices up. And, at the other extreme, in 1975, an April price rise of +25.69% was followed by +1.19%, +1.33% and +5.81% in the first three quarters of May. The markets simply ran out of steam in the short-run because of the enormous rally that had just taken place.

Chapter Seven – June 1995

> The best way for investors to earn a small fortune in June is to start with a large fortune. It is the year's worst month. A £1,000 June investment, from 1919 to 1993, would have shrunk to £552.
>
> Like May, June prices rise in most years but occasional Big Hits wipe out years' worth of accumulated profits. Big Hits seem to occur when share prices have been rising very sharply and the market is over-heated, or when the price trend is weak.

June is the worst month of the year in which to own shares. Between 1919 and 1993, prices fell at an average rate of -0.66%, equal to 22 points on a 3300 FT-SE 100.

June has a poor record

This poor record is not just a recent trend. Going back through history, it was 12th-ranked in 1919–43, the first 25 years of our historical record.

The trend seemingly improved in the 1980s. Prices rose +1.81% per year with a record of seven up and three down. But the rise was more a function of broad trading conditions affecting all months, rather than an improvement in June's relative strength, as June was ranked eighth-best month during this period (*see Table 7.1*).

As far as the 1990s is concerned, the record is two up and two down. The average loss of -1.91% over the past four years places June, once again, in 12th place on the monthly profit rankings for the current decade.

Big Hits

Given this dismal record, it may surprise you to learn that, like May, June prices rise in slightly more than half of all years. Also, like May, the first quarter of the month tends to be profitable. The losses occur in the second to fourth segments of the month.

The major problem for the June investor is the imbalance between the size of up versus down-moves. Since records began, there have been 14 declines of 5.00% or more versus just four increases of that magnitude. A Big Hit seems to pop up every five or six years on average. Simply put, the pain provided by losing years is greater then the pleasure provided by winning years.

Table 7.1

JUNE PRICE RISES AND DECLINES: 1919–1993

	Average June price change	Up	Down
1920–29	-1.39%	4	6
1930–39	0.79%	6	4
1940–49	-2.93%	5	5
1950–59	1.45%	7	3
1960–69	-1.20%	4	6
1970–79	-2.79%	3	7
1980–89	1.81%	7	3
1990–93	-1.91%	2	2
Average June price change	-0.66%	39	36

Table 7.1: June is the year's worst month for investors despite the fact that share prices rise more than 50% of the time. The key problem is that big drops of 5% or more occur every five or six years on average. Fortunately, there are ways to pin-point when Big Hits are most likely to occur.

Avoid Big Hits

If there were a way of avoiding Big Hit years, long-term June investors would profit handsomely. They would still encounter some losing years but the winners would more than compensate for those 'normal' sized losers. Our historical record shows that Big Hit years are well sign-posted in the run-up to June. Big Hits have never appeared if *any* of these conditions has occurred.[1]

Time frame	Trend	Number of years	Number of Big Hits
December–May	0.00% to +11.57%	27	0
March–May	+1.11% to +4.81%	14	0
April–May	+5.13% to +10.57%	17	0
May	+2.43% to +6.01%	15	0

[1] Reminder: All monthly calculations are based on the FT-Non-Financial Index, formerly the FT-'500'; unless otherwise stated, they are based on data from 1919–1993. All daily, quarterly, and bi-monthly calculations are based on the Ordinary Share Index, also known as the FT-30; unless otherwise stated, they are based on data from 1936-1993.

Even fractions of a percent count

In using these signals, resist the temptation to round off to the nearest whole percent. Fractions of a percent count. Take the May rule for example: There were two years close to but just below the 'safety zone', a +2.04% May increase in 1985 and a +2.00% increase in 1992. June prices fell by -6.72% and -7.58% in those two years. Imagine your pain if you modified the rule and held shares in those two years because you considered any May increase in the area of 2% to be a safe signal.

There is a good deal of overlap between these safety zones. In total, there have been 41 years touched by at least one of them. A Big Hit has not occurred in any of them. The typical profit in a 'safe' year is +1.16%, equal to about 38 points on a FT-SE 100 in the area of 3300. Could a Big Hit occur in the future in a so-called safe year? Of course. But it hasn't happened yet (*see Figure 7.1*).

The common element linking each time frame is that Big Hits do not seem to occur when share prices are rising at a comfortable rate. The odds of one occurring increase when markets rise too strongly and become overheated, rise very weakly, or fall in the run-up to June.

Figure 7.1

JUNE MONTHLY PRICE TREND: 1919–1993

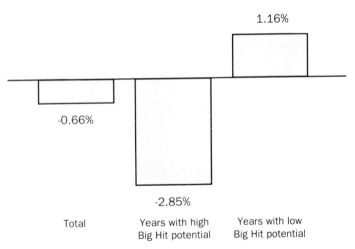

Figure 7.1: It is dangerous to hold shares when a Big Hit warning flashes. But in other years, profits are likely. The warning signals in the run-up to Big Hit Junes are on page 95.

In the 34 years outside of these safety ranges, the June record has been simply awful. A Big Hit has occurred 14 times or 41% of the time. Prices fell by less than 5% in eight other years and rose just 12 times (or 35% of the time) resulting in an average loss of -2.85%, equal to 94 points on a FT-SE 100 of 3300.

Here are some other ways to tell if this is a Big Hit year.

Back-to-back
Big Hits

▶ If a Big Hit is experienced in May, the odds are small that one will also occur in June. Out of 14 May Big Hits, two were followed by a June Big Hit. One was in 1940, during the darkest days of the war when there was a real risk we might lose. June prices fell -22.10% after a May fall of -11.60%. The other exception was in the worst stretch of the 1973 –74 Bear Market, the spring of 1974, when prices fell -19.55% in March, -8.08% in May and -10.48% in June. So, unless market conditions are catastrophically poor, the odds of back-to-back Big Hits in May and June are quite low.

▶ Since 1936, when daily indices were first published in the United Kingdom, there have been 11 June Big Hit years. In nine of them, prices fell during the first quarter of June. The two exceptions were in the tumultuous years of 1974 and 1975 when Big Hits occurred despite the first-quarter price rise. As a rough rule of thumb, if the first-quarter price trend is up, it is likely that June will not be subjected to a Big Hit. Prices might fall, but by less than 5%.

▶ The third backup signal to watch is the direction of prices in the second half of May. Nine of the 11 post-1936 Big Hits occurred after a price decline on the FT-Ordinary Share Index (the FT-30). The two exceptions: 1992 when second-half prices rose by just +0.04%, the equivalent of one point on the FT-SE 100 and in the atypical 1975. Implication: If prices rise in the second half of May, a Big Hit is not very likely, even if one of the price trends listed on page 95 flashed a warning signal.

June price drops

Even if Big Hits are not expected, it is still possible for share prices to fall. Investors must pick their time carefully to avoid a money-losing June. One price trend that does a very good job of tipping when June's prices will fall is the direction of prices in the preceding 12 months (June 1st to May 31st). If prices have fallen in the preceding 12 months by any amount, and have fallen between -0.06% to -11.88% in the past six months, June prices will probably fall. Out of 11 years which followed this scenario, June prices fell in 10 of those years. Five of the 10 were Big Hits.

Rose (1)

Fell (10)

June record after a preceding 12-month fall and a six-month fall of -0.06% to -11.88%.

The message to long term investors is quite clear. Despite June's poor reputation, it is safe to invest in June if you pick your years carefully. You will make money in two out of three years.

FIRST QUARTER OF JUNE – JUNE 1ST TO JUNE 8TH

Although June is often terrible for investors, the first quarter has been a consistent money-maker. The last bad stretch ran from 1961 to 1972 when first-quarter prices fell in 10 out of 12 years. But things suddenly changed for the better. From 1973 to the present, prices rose in 16 of 21 years at an average rate of +1.30% per year (*see Table 7.2*).

Despite the fact that the first quarter tends to be profitable, our analysis of share price trends on a day-by-day basis reveals that the first few trading days tend to be money-losers in most years. June 6–7 are quite profitable, especially June 6th which rises 69% of the time. It is the ninth most profitable day of the entire year, quite surprising for so poor a month (*see Figure 7.2*).

Table 7.2

PERCENTAGE PRICE CHANGE JUNE: 1936–1993

	June 1–8	June 9–15	June 16–23	June 24–30
Average annual price change				
1936–39	-0.22%	-1.30%	1.39%	-0.13%
1940–49	-0.49%	-0.09%	-1.71%	-0.18%
1950–59	0.94%	0.00%	0.86%	-0.56%
1960–69	-0.53%	-0.56%	-0.84%	0.81%
1970–79	0.55%	-3.09%	-0.59%	-0.76%
1980–89	1.47%	0.16%	0.17%	-0.09%
1990–93	0.03%	0.62%	-0.62%	-1.80%
Average quarterly price change	0.32%	-0.66%	-0.31%	-0.27%
Number of years in which prices:				
rose	33	24	28	27
fell	24	34	29	30
remained unchanged	1	–	1	1

Table 7.2: The first quarter is the month's only profitable segment. The next three tend to be losers, especially the second quarter, which is the year's worst performer.

Thursday, June 8th

Prices rise on the final day of the quarter, June 8th, exactly 50% of the time. Unfortunately, history also hints of a persistent price weakness on the second Thursday of June, a trend that has been operative for almost six decades. We choose our words carefully by reporting a 'hint' of a trend. Statistically, the data is flimsy because of the small number of observations. Nevertheless, what caught our eye was the fact that on four consecutive days, June 8–11, prices rise less often when the day lands on a Thursday. For readers more comfortable with solid, statistically significant findings, we will be happy to oblige – in another half-century or so, assuming it is a trend and it hasn't changed by then. For readers who do not have the inclination to wait that long, here is the evidence accumulated to date.

Figure 7.2

PERCENTAGE OF TIME PRICES RISE EACH TRADING DAY IN JUNE'S FIRST QUARTER

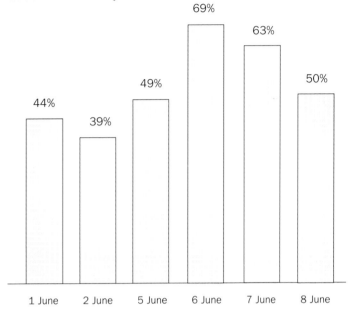

Figure 7.2: Although the first quarter is profitable in most years, it does not pay to buy shares at the very beginning of the quarter. If you do plan to buy or sell shares, be sure to factor the strength of June 6 and 7 into your thinking, especially June 6, the year's ninth-best day. June 8 tends to do poorly when it falls on a Thursday as in 1995.

LIKELIHOOD OF A PRICE RISE ON JUNE 8 – 11

	Thursday		Other day of week	
	Number of days	Percent of time prices rose	Number of days	Percent of time prices rose
June 8	8	38%	34	53%
June 9	8	38%	34	47%
June 10	9	22%	31	45%
June 11	9	33%	32	50%
4-day total	34	32%	131	49%

We offer no theory to explain why mid-month Thursdays are weak but caution readers that June 8th will land on a Thursday in 1995. Given the general rate of rising prices at that time of the month, a 32% rate of increase for Thursday seems low.

Looking at the overall first-quarter trend, there are several historical relationships that increase the odds of correctly forecasting which way prices will move.

Watch for Big Hit signals

One important signal to watch out for is the possibility of a Big Hit using one of the monthly signals discussed earlier. If 1995 turns out to be a potential Big Hit month, the odds are high that first-quarter prices will fall, even if no monthly Big Hit occurs. Since 1936, out of 23 years classified as being a possible Big Hit June, first-quarter prices fell 16 times (70%). But if no Big Hit is forecast, there is a 74% probability of turning a first-quarter profit (*see Figure 7.3*).

In months with a low probability of a Big Hit, the odds of a first-quarter profit are especially high if prices rose in May's fourth quarter by +0.27% to +1.51%. Out of 10 years with a May price move in the designated range, first-quarter prices rose each time.

Figure 7.3

STOCK MARKET TREND IN JUNE'S FIRST QUARTER: 1936–1993

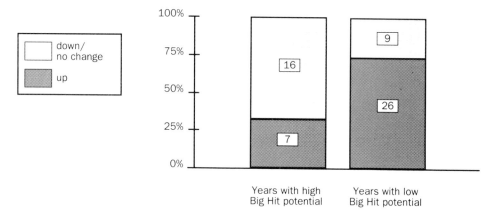

Figure 7.3: In years with a high likelihood of a Big Hit, stand aside. Prices fall 70% of the time. But first-quarter prices rise 74% of the time in safe years.

Rose (10)

Fell (0) |

First-quarter record after a price rise of +0.27 % to +1.51% in May's fourth quarter (in 'safe' years)

May price signals   Another trend that tips first-quarter prices is the direction of prices during the month of May. This trend is operative in all years, regardless of the Big Hit potential. If May prices rise moderately, first-quarter prices will probably rise too. There have been 10 occasions since 1936 when May prices rose by +2.47% to +3.96%. June's first quarter rose in nine of those years. The single exception was in 1971.

Rose (9)

Fell (1)

First-quarter record after a price rise of +2.47% to +3.96% in May

Another way to forecast the direction of first-quarter prices is to study May's fourth-quarter price trend. We originally reported this trend in the *1994 Investor's Diary*. Here's an improved update. If share prices rise by +0.64% to +1.51% during May's fourth quarter, price increases usually occur in June's first quarter. Out of 10 years when May activity followed this trend, June's first quarter rose nine times.

Rose (9)

Fell (1)

First-quarter record after a price rise of +0.64% to +1.51% in May's fourth quarter

If you watch the price trend during May's second half, it is also possible to pin-point years when prices are especially likely to fall. The losses are often large enough to give speculators a short-term opportunity to profit by betting against the market.

May's second half

Since 1948, there have been 14 years with a decline in the second half of May of under -5.00% and a fourth-quarter decline of -0.20% to -2.98%. Prices fell in June's first quarter in 12 of those years (86%). The average loss during those 14 years was -1.30%.

Rose (2)

Fell (12)

First-quarter record after a price fall of up to -5.00% in May's second half and fourth-quarter price fall of -0.20% to -2.98% (since 1948)

And if prices rise in the second half of May, with fourth-quarter prices fluctuating within a range of -2.79% to +1.51%, first-quarter prices will probably rise. Out of 12 times with price moves within this range, first-quarter prices rose 10 times.

Rose (10)

Fell (2)

First-quarter record after a price rise in May's second half and fourth-quarter price shift of -2.79% to +1.51%

SECOND QUARTER OF JUNE – JUNE 9TH TO JUNE 15TH

The average share price in the second quarter of June drops -0.66% each year, the worst quarterly performance of the year. The quarter is second-lowest in terms of the percentage of time in which prices rise (41%). Even during the 1980s' Bull Market decade, the record was four up, six down and an average increase of +0.16%. Subtract the +6.53% increase of 1980 – the largest increase ever realised in June's second quarter – and this decade also would have been a loser for investors (*see Table 7.3*).

Table 7.3   **PERCENTAGE PRICE CHANGE FOR JUNE SINCE 1980**

	June 1–8	June 9–15	June 16–23	June 24–30
1980	3.03%	6.53%	2.91%	-0.64%
1981	1.00%	-0.02%	-0.60%	0.06%
1982	1.14%	-3.89%	-2.64%	-0.27%
1983	0.31%	0.11%	1.31%	-0.58%
1984	4.33%	-1.88%	-0.50%	0.76%
1985	-0.09%	-2.25%	-1.62%	-2.55%
1986	1.19%	-1.74%	1.86%	2.16%
1987	0.88%	3.44%	-1.96%	1.77%
1988	1.94%	2.09%	0.75%	-0.90%
1989	0.99%	-0.80%	2.21%	-0.73%
1990	2.03%	1.75%	-0.67%	-0.68%
1991	-0.10%	1.08%	-1.47%	-3.56%
1992	-2.69%	-1.50%	-1.47%	-2.72%
1993	0.88%	1.16%	1.13%	-0.22%
Average quarterly price change				
1980–89	1.47%	0.16%	0.17%	-0.09%
1980–93	1.06%	0.29%	-0.05%	-0.58%
Number of years in which prices:				
rose	11	7	6	4
fell	3	7	8	10

Table 7.3: First-quarter prices have risen in 11 of the past 14 years. The trend for the other three segments steadily worsens. The fourth-quarter trend is especially weak, dropping six consecutive times since the 1987 crash.

Analysis of prices on a day-to-day basis reveals a poor pattern, but no worse than many other segments of the year (*see Figure 7.4*). Why, then, is this quarter the year's biggest loser? Is it because of the size of the average daily loss, driven higher by the occasional Big Hits that periodically strike June?

As with the first quarter, an important signal to watch for is the possibility of a Big Hit. If 1995 turns out to be a potentially dangerous month, there is a 70% chance that second-quarter

Figure 7.4

PERCENTAGE OF TIME PRICES RISE EACH TRADING DAY IN JUNE'S SECOND QUARTER

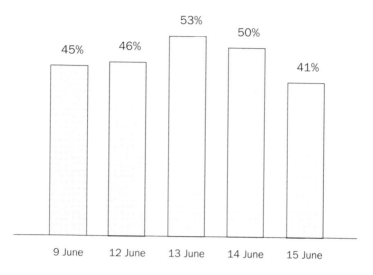

Figure 7.4: This is the year's least profitable quarter. The odds favour standing aside during this segment of the month unless a unique situation arises.

prices will fall. Unless you feel very positive about market conditions in such a year, it would be a good time to stand aside. But if no Big Hit is forecast, there is roughly a 50:50 chance of turning a second-quarter profit (*see Figure 7.5*).

Invest selectively for consistent profit

Clearly, the only way to profit consistently in the second quarter is to invest selectively when market conditions are favourable. To help you improve the odds of a profitable investment, the market sends several useful signals. One of the best is the interaction between May's fourth quarter and June's first quarter. In the *1994 Investor's Diary*, we reported on several correlations involving these two periods. Here is an update.

If weak prices in May's fourth quarter are followed by strong prices in June's first quarter, look out. Second-quarter prices will probably fall once the first quarter up-move is finished. Here is the evidence. There have been 16 years when the price of the average share fell in May's fourth quarter,

Figure 7.4   **STOCK MARKET TREND IN JUNE'S SECOND QUARTER: 1936–1993**

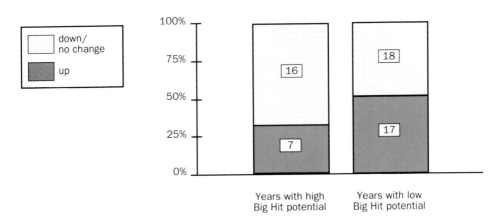

Figure 7.5: The risk of a second-quarter loss is very high if any Big Hit warning signals have flashed at the beginning of the month. But even in the best of times, there is a 50:50 chance of turning a profit.

or rose by no more than +0.27%, and rose in the first quarter by at least +0.18%. Second-quarter prices declined in 13 of these years (81%). The average quarterly decline during those 16 years was -1.25%, equal to 41 points on an FT-SE 100 in the area of 3300.

Rose (3)

Fell (13)

Second-quarter record after a price shift in May's fourth quarter of +0.27% or less and a first-quarter price rise of at least +0.18%

On the other hand, if the first-quarter price rise of at least +0.18% is preceded with a May fourth-quarter price rise of +0.64% to +2.90%, prices will probably continue to rise in the second quarter. Second-quarter prices rose in 11 out of 12 years with the two prior price trends in the appropriate range. The sole exception was in 1953. The average second-quarter increase is +1.07%.

Rose (11)

Fell (1)

Second-quarter record after a price rise in May's fourth quarter of +0.64% to +2.90% and a first-quarter price rise of at least +0.18%

Another signal to watch for is a decline of -0.60% to -2.69% in June's first quarter. If prices fall in this range, the odds are good that they will continue to fall in the second quarter. Out of 13 occasions since 1936 when share prices fell within this range in the first quarter, second-quarter prices declined 11 times (85%). The average decline during those years was -2.16%. That's equal to 71 points on an FT-SE 100 in the area of 3300.

Rose (2)

Fell (11)

Second-quarter record after a price drop in June's first quarter of -0.60% to -2.69%

THIRD QUARTER OF JUNE – JUNE 16TH TO JUNE 23RD

Investors typically lose money by investing during the third quarter. Between 1936 and 1992, the third quarter of June rose 48% of the time and generated an average loss of -0.31% per year. The profit picture may not be as grim as for the second quarter but it's not good.

The price trend has continued to show weakness during the last few decades. Share prices fell in the 1960s and '70s. In the Bull Market 1980s, the record was five up and five down, and an average yearly share price increase of +0.17%, less than the rate of return at your local building society. The record for the 1990s, so far, is three out of four declines.

The quarter's
best day

The first trading day is the quarter's best day. Prices rise 57% of the time on the 16th, a pattern that has been holding firm for six decades. During the last 10 years, shares rose five out of six times (weekends account for the missing days) (*see Figure 7.6*). Unfortunately, 1995 may be an exception. There is a long-standing tendency for prices to be weak on mid-June Fridays. Since 1936, June 15th, 16th, or 17th have landed on a Friday 24 times. Prices rose on seven of those days (29%). These same three days rise 52% of the time when they land on a Monday to Thursday. 16 June 1995 is a Friday.

Once again, a critical signal is the monthly Big Hit signal. If 1995 turns out to be a 'high potential' Big Hit month, the odds are high (65%) that third-quarter prices will fall. But if no Big Hit is forecast, there is a slightly better than even chance (57%) of turning a third-quarter profit (*see Figure 7.7*).

Figure 7.6

PERCENTAGE OF TIME PRICES RISE EACH TRADING DAY IN JUNE'S THIRD QUARTER

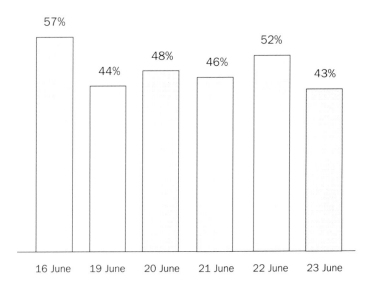

Figure 7.6: Another poor segment of the month. In most years, it makes sense to stand aside. The best day of the quarter is June 16. But this year, June 16 lands on a Friday and prices often fall on mid-month Fridays.

Figure 7.7

STOCK MARKET TREND IN JUNE'S THIRD QUARTER: 1936–1993

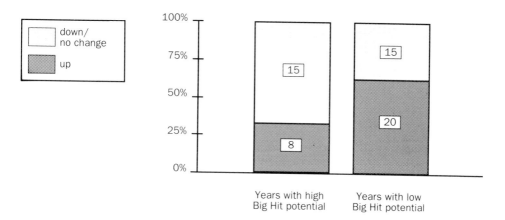

Figure 7.7: There is a big risk of a third-quarter fall if any of the Big Hit warning signals flash at the beginning of the month.

Down-side bets

If you are betting on the down-side, one way to increase your odds of success is to watch second-quarter prices. If they fall by -1.23% or more, the odds of a third-quarter decline increase. Since 1973, second-quarter prices fell within this range 10 times. In nine of them, the fall was immediately followed by a decline in the third quarter. The average loss was -2.29%, equal to 76 points on a 3300 FT-SE 100.

Rose (1)

Fell (9)

Third-quarter record after a price drop in June's second quarter of at least -1.23% (since 1973)

Another trend to watch is the direction of prices in the first half of June. If they fall by -2.79% to -6.83%, the odds are high that prices will also decline in the third quarter. Out of 13 years in which first-half prices fell within the defined range, the third quarter declined 10 times. Two of the exceptions were in 1970 when the Conservatives won a mid-June election (third-quarter prices rose +10.68%) and 1971 when the markets got wind of a July tax cut. These exceptions confirm the point that news-making events can overwhelm even the strongest of trends. If you put these two atypical years aside for the moment, a first-half drop in share prices within a range of -2.79% to -6.83% is associated with a third-quarter drop in 10 out of 11 years.

Rose (3)

Fell (10)

Third-quarter record after a price drop in June's first half of -2.79% to -6.83% (two exceptional years included)

Large declines likely

Large price declines also often occur in years when prices decline in the second half of May and first half of June. Out of 16 years in which prices declined in both periods, by at least -0.33% in May and -0.77% in June, the third quarter declined 13 times (81%), by an average of -2.34% per year. In 1937, one of the three exceptions, third-quarter prices rose by just +0.09%.

Rose (3)

Fell (13)

Third-quarter record after a price drop in May's second half by at least -0.33% and June's first half by at least -0.77%

There are two rays of sunshine in this cloudy investment climate. If June's second quarter rises by +1.09% to +2.50%, third-quarter prices will probably rise. Out of 11 second-quarter shifts within this range, June's third quarter rose nine times. Unfortunately, the average gain was just +0.63%.

Rose (9)

Fell (2)

Third-quarter record after a price rise in June's second quarter of +1.09% to +2.50%

If June's first *and* second quarters rise, with the second quarter rising between +0.11% to +1.57%, the third quarter often also rises. Out of 11 years when both preceding quarters rose within the designated range, the third quarter rose nine times (82%). The average rise was +1.56%. The two exceptions to the rule were back in 1944 and 1946.

Rose (9)

Fell (2)

Third-quarter record after a price rise in June's first quarter of any amount and a second-quarter rise of +0.11% to +1.57%

Caution!

For readers dreaming of big short-term profits, one note of caution. Keep in mind that prices almost always drop in any June fourth quarter that follows three ups. So act quickly.

FOURTH QUARTER OF JUNE – JUNE 24TH TO JUNE 30TH

The fourth quarter of June offers poor investment potential. In the long-run, investors have lost money by consistently investing during the fourth quarter. The only profitable decade on record was the 1960s. The price trend is weakest at the beginning of the quarter, especially June 27th which falls 60% of the time (*see Figure 7.8*).

Between 1936 and 1992, the fourth quarter of June rose 47% of the time and generated an average loss of -0.27%. The record since the 1987 crash is six declines in a row, leaving June's fourth quarter tied with one other quarter as the worst performer of the year.

111

Figure 7.8

PERCENTAGE OF TIME PRICES RISE EACH TRADING DAY IN JUNE'S FOURTH QUARTER

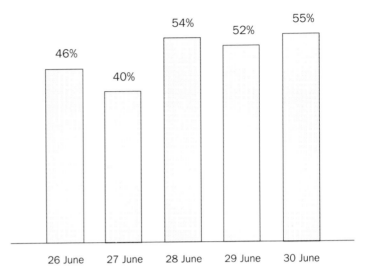

Figure 7.8: The quarter starts off slowly. If you are planning to buy shares, the odds suggest holding off until late in the day on June 27.

Watch for signals

Big Hits don't seem to affect this quarter as badly as they do other quarters. Prices rise 48% of the time in 'high potential' Big Hit years, and 46% in 'low potential' years (*see Figure 7.9*). But the absence of a Big Hit signal at the beginning of the month does send one useful market-timing signal. In years with a low likelihood of a Big Hit, if third-quarter prices rose +1.13% to +4.18%, fourth-quarter prices fell nine out of 10 times.

Rose (1)

Fell (9)

Fourth-quarter record in low risk years after a third-quarter price rise of +1.13% to +4.18%

Despite the unexciting general market conditions, we find two good price signals, one tipping up-moves and one tipping down-moves, which are operative in all fourth quarters. If prices rise in the first half of June by no more than +2.92%, and shift in the third quarter within a range of -1.24% to +0.53%, fourth-quarter prices will probably rise. There have been 12 years with price shifts within this range. Fourth-quarter prices rose in 11 of those years. The single exception was back in 1950.

Rose (11)

Fell (1)

Fourth-quarter record after a price rise in June's first half by no more than +2.92% and shift in the third quarter of -1.24% to +0.53%

A trend is developing

We first reported in the *1994 Investor's Diary* a tendency for prices to fall in the fourth quarter if they rise in June's first, second, and third quarters. It happened again in 1993. Here is the rule that seems to be developing. There have been eight years in which prices rose in the three preceding quarters, with a third-quarter rise of at least +0.50%. Fourth-quarter prices fell in each of those years. The average annual decline was -1.12%.

Rose (0)

Fell (8)

Fourth-quarter record after a price rise in three consecutive quarters, with a third-quarter rise of at least +0.50%.

Figure 7.9   **STOCK MARKET TREND IN JUNE'S FOURTH QUARTER: 1936–1993**

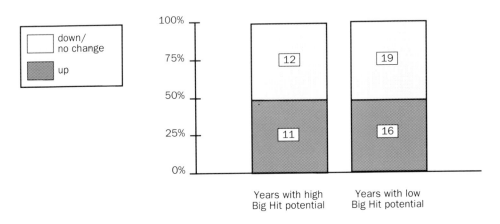

Figure 7.9: It is hard to profit consistently in the fourth quarter. It is a good time to stand on the sidelines unless you have reason to believe this year will be different.

CHAPTER EIGHT – JULY 1995

July is a poor month to be in the market on a consistent basis. Shares do rise on average, but only by a tiny amount. The best years for the July investor were prior to the 1960s. Since then, this month has produced a sorry record. Big profits do occur occasionally. But you must pick the right moment. Be warned: unlike other poor months, for example May, June, and September, prices are weak in the first quarter of July as well as for the rest of the month.

July is ranked eighth in terms of monthly profitability. The July investor typically makes a small profit. Between 1919 and 1993, prices rose at a yearly average of just +0.22%, equal to slightly over seven points on a 3300 FT-SE 100. A start-up investment of £1,000, placed in shares each July from 1919 to 1993, and in cash for the rest of each year, would have grown to just £1,103. If the same sum were deposited into a risk-free building society savings account each July, earning an average of 4% per year (on an annual basis), it would have grown to £1,284 by 1993.

A poor month for investors

Worse still, the best decades for the July investor were prior to 1960. Since then, the trend has weakened. The average return was -2.28% in the 1960s, and -0.18% in the 1970s (*see Table 8.1*).

In the Bull Market 1980s, July returned to the profit column. Note though, that the average annual increase of +0.64% merely reached ninth place on the monthly profitability rankings. And most of this profit was due to 1989 when prices rose by +6.10%.

In the last 20 years, the July record was the worst of all 12 months – nine up and 11 down. Even June did better with a record of 10 up and 10 down.

Despite the poor record, investors can profit if they invest selectively and nimbly. Several historical price trends provide good insight into the expected direction of prices.

A good signal to watch for is a small price shift, in either direction, in the first half of the year. If prices have fluctuated

Table 8.1   **JULY PRICE RISES AND DECLINES: 1919–1993**

	Average July price change	Up	Down
1920–29	-0.86%	5	5
1930–39	1.51%	6	4
1940–49	2.20%	6	4
1950–59	0.73%	6	4
1960–69	-2.28%	4	6
1970–79	-0.18%	4	6
1980–89	0.64%	6	4
1990–93	-0.09%	2	2
Average July price change	0.22%	39	36

Table 8.1: July is a lacklustre month, especially in the recent past. The three most profitable decades were prior to 1960. Even in the Bull Market 1980s, its +0.64% profit was merely ninth-ranked.

---

in January to June by -2.22% to + 9.85%, and in the preceding two months within a range of -1.98% to +4.25%, July prices will probably rise.[1] Out of 16 years which followed this scenario, July prices rose 15 times.

Rose (15)

Fell (1)

July's record after a previous six-month price shift of -2.22% to +9.85% and a previous two-month shift of -1.98% to +4.25%

May/June signal   Since 1961, a price decline of at least -5.10% during May and June signals that July prices will probably fall. Out of 12 years with this price trend in the run-up to July, prices fell 11 times.

---

[1] Reminder: All monthly calculations are based on the FT-Non-Financial Index, formerly the FT-'500'; unless otherwise stated, they are based on data from 1919–1993. All daily, quarterly, and bi-monthly calculations are based on the Ordinary Share Index, also known as the FT-30; unless otherwise stated, they are based on data from 1935-1993.

Rose (1) ☐

Fell (11) ☐

July's record after a drop of -5.10% or more during May and June (since 1961)

The three months ahead

A price decline within the range of -5.00% to -9.99% during May and June has even more far-reaching implications. Out of 15 such occasions since 1919, prices were still lower on September 30th, or had risen by less than 1% 11 times. Two of the exceptional years produced moderate increases: +2.37% in 1956 and +6.22% in 1965. The two very big exceptions to the rule were +13.51% in 1975 and +9.82% in 1984. The common element linking these two big increases was a brief May/June price retraction during an enormously powerful Bull Market.

Put it all together: unless you are in the middle of a very powerful Bull Market, a May/June decline of 5–10% signals poor odds of making a profit for the entire third quarter of the year, not just for July. More money will be made, in the long-run, by depositing your funds in a building society savings account.

Large rise (2) ☐

Medium rise (2) ☐

Small rise
or fall (11) ☐

Third-quarter record after a drop of -5.00% to -9.99% during May and June

FIRST QUARTER OF JULY – JULY 1ST TO JULY 8TH

At first glance, the first quarter looks to be a profitable time period in which to invest. The record since 1935 is 32 up months (54%), 24 down months, three unchanged and an average profit of +0.46% per year. Unfortunately, many of the profits realised during this period were achieved in 1935–1959. In the past few decades, a first-quarter investor has been a consistent money-loser (see Table 8.2).

In the 1960s, first-quarter prices rose just three times. The profits of the 1970s were entirely due to an +11.86% increase in the abnormal year of 1975. On July 1st of that year, Denis Healey electrified the markets by warning unions he would introduce wage controls unless they voluntarily reduced their

Table 8.2

PERCENTAGE PRICE CHANGE JULY: 1935–1993

	July 1–8	July 9–15	July 16–23	July 24–31
Average annual price change				
1935–39	0.65%	-0.46%	0.66%	0.80%
1940–49	1.77%	0.34%	0.21%	-1.13%
1950–59	1.07%	0.08%	0.06%	-0.50%
1960–69	-0.52%	-0.91%	-0.52%	-1.27%
1970–79	0.67%	1.00%	-1.28%	-1.16%
1980–89	-0.04%	0.28%	-0.71%	0.80%
1990–93	-1.41%	0.99%	-0.48%	0.54%
Average quarterly price change	0.46%	0.16%	-0.36%	-0.45%
Number of years in which prices:				
rose	32	34	27	29
fell	24	25	32	30
remained unchanged	3	–	–	–

Table 8.2: At first glance, the first quarter looks to be the month's most profitable segment, but its performance has been relatively poor in the past few decades. The profit of the 1970s was due to a +11.86% increase in 1975. The second quarter has been the stronger of the two in the recent past. The third and fourth quarters are often money-losers.

wage demands. Share prices exploded upwards. The record for the rest of the decade was three up and six down, and an average annual loss of -0.57%.

In the Bull Market 1980s, the first quarter lost, on average -0.04% per year. And the 1990s, too, have started off poorly. The score to date is one up and three down.

Wall Street's effect on July 3rd

Analysis of daily price trends over the long-run reveals a pattern of profitable trading conditions throughout the quarter, with the exception of July 3rd (*see Figure 8.1*).

We hypothesise that July 3rd's weakness is related to Wall Street being closed on July 4th each year. American investors tend to stretch the period around July Fourth into a four- or five-day holiday. The number of people walking on Wall Street on Monday, July 3rd, and in the City on Boxing Day have a lot in common. July 3rd prices tend to be weak on Wall Street too, with very low volume.

If there is one thing Americans hate, it's a year in which July 4th lands on a Saturday as it ruins their excuse for a long weekend. British investors should be pleased though. Friday, July 3rd prices rise in most years because the normal weekend break is in effect. Unfortunately, July 3rd lands on a Monday in 1995.

For the quarter as a whole, there are ways to improve the odds of a profitable investment. A positive price trend is often tipped by the direction of prices in June's third and fourth quarters. We first called attention to this in the *1994 Investor's Diary*. Here's an improved update.

Watch June's prices

Since 1936, an increase in share prices in both quarters has been frequently associated with an increase during July's first quarter. Out of 11 years in which prices rose by at least +0.09% in the third quarter and at least +0.27% in the fourth quarter, first-quarter prices rose 10 times (91%). The average increase was +0.98%.

Rose (10)

Fell (1)

First-quarter record after a rise of at least +0.09% in June's third quarter and at least +0.27% in June's fourth quarter

119

Figure 8.1

PERCENTAGE OF TIME PRICES RISE EACH TRADING DAY IN JULY'S FIRST QUARTER

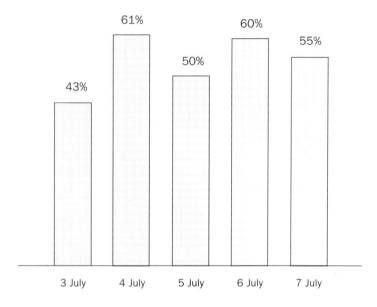

Figure 8.1: July 3rd is the quarter's weakest trading day. One exception to the rule: prices often rise when the 3rd lands on a Friday. Unfortunately, it lands on a Monday in 1995.

Since 1948, there were 11 years in which prices dropped in both June quarters by a small amount, no more than -2.79% in the third quarter and no more than -2.72% in the fourth quarter. July's first quarter rose two times and one was an increase of just +0.29%. In other words, prices rose by a reasonable margin in just one out of 11 years.

Rose (2)

Fell (8)

No change (1)

First-quarter record after a fall of up to -2.79% in June's third quarter and of up to -2.72% in June's fourth quarter (since 1948)

SECOND QUARTER OF JULY – JULY 9TH TO JULY 15TH

Although the month as a whole is not all that good to investors, the second quarter tends to be profitable. The only decade on record in which the average share dropped in value each year was back in the 1960s. Since 1970, the second-quarter record is 14 up (58%) and 10 down, and an average increase of +0.70% per year. The recent record remains profitable. Since 1990, prices have risen three out of four times (*see Table 8.3*).

Table 8.3

PERCENTAGE PRICE CHANGE FOR JULY SINCE 1980

	July 1–8	July 9–15	July 16–23	July 24–31
1980	5.55%	1.44%	-2.76%	0.88%
1981	-4.11%	1.32%	-2.02%	1.83%
1982	-0.52%	0.91%	3.92%	-3.75%
1983	-5.11%	-0.04%	3.39%	0.62%
1984	0.17%	-5.93%	-2.00%	4.66%
1985	1.34%	-1.47%	-1.72%	2.39%
1986	-3.61%	-1.15%	-1.21%	-1.15%
1987	2.50%	4.45%	-3.80%	0.89%
1988	1.59%	-0.62%	-1.21%	0.63%
1989	1.80%	3.84%	0.34%	1.01%
1990	-1.84%	0.81%	-0.69%	-1.21%
1991	0.71%	3.16%	2.82%	-0.11%
1992	-2.64%	0.27%	-4.65%	-0.24%
1993	-1.90%	-0.28%	0.59%	3.71%
Average quarterly price change				
1980–89	-0.04%	0.28%	-0.71%	0.80%
1980–93	-0.43%	0.48%	-0.64%	0.73%
Number of years in which prices:				
rose	7	8	5	9
fell	7	6	9	5

Table 8.3: The first and third quarters have been weak in recent years. The second and fourth quarters have produced profits. Unfortunately, most fourth-quarter profits were accrued in the 1980s. Prices have risen just once in the 1990s.

Figure 8.2

PERCENTAGE OF TIME PRICES RISE EACH TRADING DAY IN JULY'S SECOND QUARTER

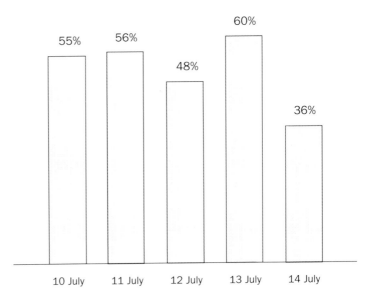

Figure 8.2: July 12 is profitable slightly less than half the time over the long-run. Unfortunately, the recent trend has weakened. In the last 10 years, prices rose once and fell six times. July 14 is the weakest day of the entire month.

Weakest day of the month

At one time, the 10th through the 13th was steadily profitable but since 1984, trading conditions on the 12th have become worse (one up and six down), pulling the long-term average down (*see Figure 8.2*). The 14th is a poor day, the weakest of the entire month. Prices rise just 36% of the time.

The market sends some useful signals to help second-quarter investors improve the odds of profiting – the direction of prices in the last half of June and the first quarter of July. If they both rise or both fall within certain limits, the odds are good that prices will rise in the second quarter.

There have been eight occasions since 1965 when the price of the average share fell in June's second half (by any amount) and July's first quarter (by at least -0.52%). Second-quarter prices rose each time.

Rose (8)

Fell (0) |

Second-quarter record after a fall in June's second half and in July's first quarter by at least -0.52% (since 1965)

There have been 11 occasions since 1952 when the price of the average share rose in June's second half (by any amount) and July's first quarter (by at least +0.84%). Second-quarter prices rose in nine of those years.

Rose (9)

Fell (2)

Second-quarter record after a rise in June's second half and in July's first quarter by at least +0.84% (since 1952)

THIRD QUARTER OF JULY – JULY 16TH TO JULY 23RD

Investors typically lose -0.36% per year by investing every third quarter. That's equal to a drop of 12 points on a 3300 FT-SE 100.

Like the first quarter of July, money was made in the 1930s, '40s, and '50s, but the trend has been poor ever since. The average share fell in value each year during the 1960s, '70s, and '80s. The record during this period was just 13 up months and 17 down.

Short-term trading opportunities

Analysis of price trends on a daily basis finds a steady pattern of red ink. The 21st of the month is especially disappointing. Prices rise just 38% of the time. Much of this weakness has occurred since 1974 when the record has been three up (21%) and 11 down (*see Figure 8.3*).

But before you get too disheartened, note that the market provides several clues which help investors to take advantage of short-term trading opportunities.

Figure 8.3

PERCENTAGE OF TIME PRICES RISE EACH TRADING DAY IN JULY'S THIRD QUARTER

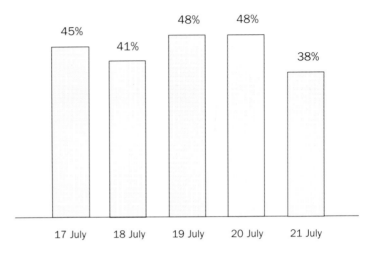

Figure 8.3: July 21 has a poor trading record. Much of this weakness has occurred since 1974 with a record of three up and 11 down.

The direction of third-quarter prices is often tipped off by the price trend of the first half of July. Prices have risen by +1.07% to +2.95% on 12 occasions. Third-quarter prices rose in 10 of those years.

Rose (10)

Fell (2)

Third-quarter record after a rise in the first half of +1.07% to +2.95%

If the second quarter moves slightly, within a range of -0.45% to +0.44%, it is a good sign that third-quarter prices will rise. Out of 12 years with a second-quarter shift within this range, third-quarter prices rose 10 times.

Rose (10)

Fell (2)

Third-quarter record after a shift in the second quarter of -0.45% to +0.44%

Watch the previous three quarters

Another signal to look out for is the trend over the previous three quarters – the last quarter of June and the first two quarters of July. If share prices steadily move in one direction during these three periods, they are likely to move in the opposite direction in the third quarter.

The average share price fell in three consecutive quarters on seven occasions since 1936. Third-quarter prices rose all seven times. The last time this signal flashed was in 1993. After a drop of over 2% in the three preceding quarters, prices rose in the third quarter.

On six other occasions, prices rose in each of the three preceding periods, with a second-quarter rise of at least +0.94%. Third-quarter prices fell each time.

What of the remaining years not preceded by three consecutive rises or declines? Here again, the market sends a pretty clear signal.

Since 1969, in years not influenced by the three prior up/three prior down rule, first-half prices fell nine times. Each of the nine falls was immediately followed by a decline in the third quarter. The average loss was a staggering -2.57%, equal to 85 points on a 3300 FT-SE 100.

Rose (0)

Fell (9)

Third-quarter record after a drop in the first half in years unaffected by the three-prior-up/three-prior-down rule (since 1969)

Fourth Quarter of July – July 24th to July 31st

The fourth quarter of July offers poor investment potential. In the long-run, investors consistently lost money by investing during the fourth quarter. The only full decade on record in which profits were made was during the Bull Market 1980s. The record for the 1990s has reverted to form with three out of four declines.

Fourth-worst segment

Between 1935 and 1993, the fourth quarter of July rose 49% of the time and generated an average loss of -0.45%, the fourth-worst quarterly performance of the entire year.

Much of the damage occurs on the 25th and 27th of the month. The other trading days of the quarter turn a profit in most years. The 28th has been especially good to investors since 1984 with a record of six ups and no downs (*see Figure 8.4*).

Figure 8.4

PERCENTAGE OF TIME PRICES RISE EACH TRADING DAY IN JULY'S FOURTH QUARTER

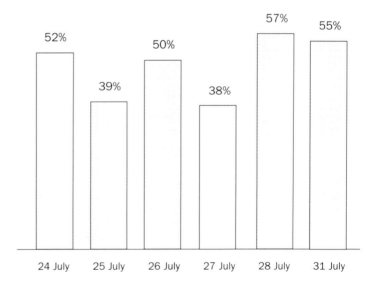

Figure 8.4: The final two trading days are the quarter's best. The 28th has been especially strong since 1984 with a record of six up and none down.

Unfortunately, we find no way to increase the odds of anticipating an up-move during this quarter of the month. But, if you are interested in betting on the down-side, here is a relationship that has been in effect since 1938. If share prices shift slightly in the first three quarters of July, no more than +0.28% on the up-side and no more than -1.49% on the down-side, they are very likely to fall in the last quarter of July. Out of 13 years with this pattern, fourth-quarter prices fell 11 times.

Rose (2)

Fell (11)

Fourth-quarter record after a shift in the first three quarters of -1.49% to +0.28% (since 1938)

Chapter Nine – August 1995

Enjoy the August sun –
miss the stock market fun

GED

> This is the third most profitable month for investors. Share prices rise +1.21% on average. It is not surprising that investors are advised: enjoy the August sun and miss the stock market fun. The first quarter is the year's third-best and the recent trend has continued to be good to investors throughout the month. But don't linger – September storm clouds hit hard in some years.

The summer slump dramatically ends with the arrival of August. Just as investors depart to sunnier climes, the market begins to rise.

Between 1919 and 1993, August prices rose 65% of the time. The average price rise was +1.21%, equal to 40 points on an FT-SE 100 in the area of 3300. Historically, August is the third-best month in which to invest in shares. A hypothetical investor who invested in August only, from 1919 to 1993, would have run up his £1,000 to £2,217.

The last losing decade for the August investor was the 1940s when prices dropped at an average annual rate of -0.32%. But under the surface, things looked pretty good even then. Prices rose in seven of the decade's 10 years. A -17.04% drop in 1947, in response to the sudden suspension of sterling's convertibility, caused all of that decade's losses.

Table 9.1

AUGUST PRICE RISES AND DECLINES: 1919–1993

	Average August price change	Up	Down/ no change
1920–29	1.59%	6	4
1930–39	-1.07%	4	6
1940–49	-0.32%	7	3
1950–59	3.12%	8	2
1960–69	2.13%	8	2
1970–79	1.42%	6	4
1980–89	2.48%	7	3
1990–93	-0.74%	2	2
Average August price change	1.21%	49	26

Table 9.1: August is the year's third-best month. The last losing decade for the August investor was back in the 1940s. Since then it has been a profitable time period for investors. A great deal of volatility has occurred in the 1990s including a price decline of -8.05% in 1990 and an increase of +6.28% in 1993.

Since then, the month has been consistently profitable. In the 1980s, prices rose in seven out of 10 years, with an average price rise of +2.48% per month, the decade's third-best performer (*see Table 9.1*).

A profitable month – but, be quick

Unfortunately, the window of opportunity that the month provides is small. The month that follows, September, is one of the worst months of the year in which to own shares. So act quickly.

... and invest selectively

Despite the good overall record, investors can make even more profit if they invest selectively.[1]

There are several historic price trends that provide good insight into the expected direction of August's prices. One of the best predictors of the August price trend is the direction of prices in the preceding 12 months.

[1] Reminder: All monthly calculations are based on the FT-Non-Financial Index, formerly the FT-'500'; unless otherwise stated, they are based on data from 1919–1993. All daily, quarterly, and bi-monthly calculations are based on the Ordinary Share Index, also known as the FT-30; unless otherwise stated, they are based on data from 1935-1993.

Watch the
12-month trend

Out of 12 years in which prices rose between +5.47% to +11.86% from September 1st to July 30th, August rose 11 times.

Rose (11)

Fell (0)

Unchanged (1)

August's record after previous 12-month price rise of +5.47% to +11.86%

Also look for price increases between +28.59% to +49.70% in the preceding September 1st to July 30th. There have been nine years with a price rise of this magnitude. August's prices rose each time.

Rose (9)

Fell (0)

August's record after previous 12-month price rise of +28.59% to +49.70%

Stock markets don't always rise, even in historically good months. Here is a useful down-side indicator for August which also utilises the price trend over the past 12 months. Since 1919, there have been seven occasions when prices fell in the preceding twelve months by -18.21% or more. August prices fell in six of those years. The single exception was in 1940, a time period heavily influenced by war-related events.

Rose (1)

Fell (6)

August's record after previous 12-month price drop of -18.21% or more

130

FIRST QUARTER OF AUGUST – AUGUST 1ST TO AUGUST 8TH

Although August is a good month in which to invest, there are widely different profit potentials associated with investments made during different segments of the month.

The best segment   The best segment is the first quarter. It has risen 68% of the time (third-best of the entire year) and produced an average annual profit in every single decade on record. Between 1935 and 1993, the average first-quarter profit was +0.91% per year, tied with the first quarter of October as the year's third-best (*see Table 9.2*).

In the 1980s and 1990s, first-quarter profitability has lagged behind the second quarter. Is this the start of a trend change? We think not. Much of the damage in the 1980s was due to 1987

Table 9.2   **PERCENTAGE PRICE CHANGE AUGUST: 1935–1993**

	August 1–8	August 9–15	August 16–23	August 24–31
Average annual price change				
1935–39	0.63%	0.28%	-2.55%	0.37%
1940–49	0.99%	0.05%	-0.11%	0.29%
1950–59	0.74%	1.02%	0.14%	0.57%
1960–69	2.12%	0.82%	0.27%	-0.09%
1970–79	1.61%	0.38%	0.22%	-0.16%
1980–89	0.10%	1.39%	0.48%	0.20%
1990–93	-1.28%	0.23%	-1.58%	0.88%
Average quarterly price change	0.91%	0.66%	-0.15%	0.23%
Number of years in which prices:				
rose	40	37	32	34
fell	18	22	27	23
remained unchanged	1	–	–	2

Table 9.2: The first-quarter trend is very strong, the year's third-best. Recent weakness is due to large declines in 1987 and 1990. The third quarter looks to be a long-term loser, but has been steadily profitable in the 1950s to 1980s.

The 3rd is the
best day

when first-quarter prices fell -6.78%. A 1990 decline of -5.20% accounts for the 1990s weakness. We shall, of course, continue to watch the situation closely.

Analysis of daily price swings shows very profitable trading conditions throughout the quarter. Prices rise 71% of the time on the 3rd of the month, the best performance of the entire month. And recent trading conditions have been especially favourable on the 1st and 8th of the month. Since 1984, prices have risen six times and fallen once on each of these days (*see Figure 9.1*).

Happily, it is possible to pin-point years with above-average prospects. Since 1941, there have been 27 years when prices shifted in the second half of July by -0.61% to +5.42%. Prices rose in August's first quarter in 24 of those years.

Rose (24)

Fell (3)

First-quarter record after a price shift of -0.61% to +5.42% in July's second half (since 1941)

In the *1994 Investor's Diary*, we pointed out the relationship between price trends in July's fourth quarter and August's first quarter. Here is an update. There have been 27 years in which fourth-quarter prices shifted -0.18% to +2.64%. Prices rose in August's first quarter in 24 of those years (89%).

Rose (24)

Fell (3)

First-quarter record after a price shift of -0.18% to +2.64% in July's fourth quarter

A good down-side indicator is a small decline in July's fourth quarter. Prices fell by -0.24% to -1.23% on 10 occasions since 1938. First-quarter prices fell still further in nine of those years.

Figure 9.1

PERCENTAGE OF TIME PRICES RISE EACH TRADING DAY IN AUGUST'S FIRST QUARTER

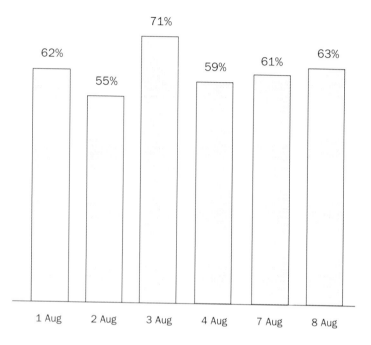

Figure 9.1: Prices often rise during this quarter of the month. The 3rd is the best day of the entire month. Share prices have risen in six of the last seven trading days on August 1st and 8th.

Rose (1)

Fell (9)

First-quarter record after a price fall of -0.24% to -1.23% in July's fourth quarter (since 1938)

SECOND QUARTER OF AUGUST – AUGUST 9TH TO AUGUST 15TH

Second-quarter prices rose 63% of the time between 1935 and 1993, slightly less often than the first quarter. Prices rose +0.66% on average, also less than the first quarter but still highly respectable.

The trend has improved since 1980. A consistent second-quarter investor received an average annual quarterly profit of +1.39% during that decade. In the last 14 years, the second quarter performed better than the first nine times (see Table 9.3).

Analysis of price trends on a day-by-day basis shows that shares rise in value more than half the time on most days in this quarter. The recent record for August 14th is especially good. Since 1984, prices rose seven times and fell just once (see Figure 9.2).

Second-quarter investors: watch for the signal

As if these results aren't good enough, the market sends a useful signal that helps second-quarter investors obtain even better returns. The signal is contained in the price trend during July's second half and August's first quarter. If shares make a steady move through both periods, regardless of direction, the second quarter will probably rise.

Since 1949, there have been 12 years in which prices rose in July's second half *and* August's first quarter. The price rise continued through August's second quarter in 10 of those years (83%). One of the two exceptions occurred in 1993 when second-quarter prices fell by a minuscule -0.01% after a steady price rise in the two preceding periods.

Rose (12)

Fell (2)

Second-quarter record after a price rise in July's second half and August's first quarter (since 1949)

There were 11 other years since 1957 in which prices fell in July's second half and August's first quarter. Prices bounced back with an increase in August's second quarter in nine of those years. And one of the exceptions to the rule, in 1990, saw a second-quarter drop of just -0.02%.

Table 9.3

PERCENTAGE PRICE CHANGE FOR AUGUST SINCE 1980

	August 1–8	August 9–15	August 16–23	August 24–31
1980	-1.88%	0.56%	3.12%	-3.01%
1981	1.87%	6.41%	-1.92%	2.19%
1982	-1.38%	-0.71%	5.80%	-0.66%
1983	1.42%	1.59%	-1.20%	-2.29%
1984	6.14%	0.31%	-0.76%	2.22%
1985	1.58%	1.95%	1.51%	2.27%
1986	-4.29%	4.40%	0.02%	3.20%
1987	-6.78%	3.38%	-3.25%	1.89%
1988	1.75%	-3.24%	0.03%	-3.87%
1989	2.63%	-0.74%	1.44%	0.09%
1990	-5.20%	-0.02%	-8.24%	5.57%
1991	1.00%	0.92%	1.31%	0.48%
1992	-2.80%	0.03%	0.09%	-4.26%
1993	1.87%	-0.01%	0.54%	1.72%
Average quarterly price change				
1980–89	0.10%	1.39%	0.48%	0.20%
1980–93	-0.29%	1.06%	-0.11%	0.40%
Number of years in which prices:				
rose	8	9	9	9
fell	6	5	5	5

Table 9.3: The recent price trend is looking good. Increases occur in most years for all four quarters. At first glance, the first-quarter trend is weak, marred by large declines in 1986, 1987, and 1990. The second quarter has pleasantly surprised investors by out-performing the first in nine out of the last 14 years. The third quarter suffered one bad hit, a -8.24% decline in 1990.

Rose (9)

Fell (2)

Second-quarter record after a price fall in July's second half and August's first quarter (since 1957)

Figure 9.2 **PERCENTAGE OF TIME PRICES RISE EACH TRADING DAY IN AUGUST'S SECOND QUARTER**

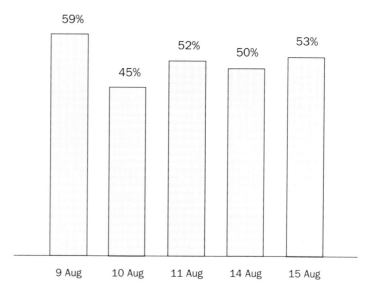

Figure 9.2: Prices rise more than half the time on most of this quarter's trading days. August 14th has been especially strong since 1984 with a record of seven up and one down.

Third Quarter of August – August 16th to August 23rd

If you slavishly follow the message portrayed by the averages, you would conclude that a steady investment every third quarter is a money-losing proposition. Over the 59 year period studied, the third quarter averaged a -0.15% loss each year.

But a closer look at the raw data tells a different story. There were big losses in the last half of the 1930s when share prices fell five years in a row, and in 1990 when the average share dropped -8.24%. In the intervening period, the results weren't all that bad – price rises in most years and average annual profits during the 1950s, '60s, '70s and '80s. In the most recent 10 years, from 1984 to 1993, prices rose seven times.

Figure 9.3

PERCENTAGE OF TIME PRICES RISE EACH TRADING DAY IN AUGUST'S THIRD QUARTER

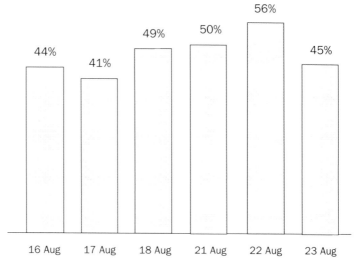

Figure 9.3: The quarter starts and ends weakly, especially August 17, the worst day of the month. But the trend improves during the middle of the quarter.

Analysis of daily price swings finds that prices are weakest on the first two days of the quarter, especially the 17th which is the worst day of the month (*see Figure 9.3*).

Look out for the second-quarter signal

Since 1967, a potentially profit-making statistical relationship has become apparent. During this period, there have been 10 years when prices dropped in August's second quarter. They bounced back with a third-quarter increase in nine of these years. The average annual increase was +0.75%. And this average was pulled down quite substantially by the sole exception to the rule, the -8.24% decline of 1990. The Second-quarter Signal last flashed in 1993 when prices rose in the third quarter after a second-quarter decline of just -0.01%.

Rose (9)

Fell (1)

Third-quarter record after a price drop in August's second quarter (since 1967)

137

A new trend

A new trend is in the process of developing. Since 1980, prices shifted in the first half of August within a range of -2.77% to +1.93%, on eight occasions. Third-quarter prices rose each time. In the remaining six years when prices shifted outside of this range, third-quarter prices fell five times.

FOURTH QUARTER OF AUGUST – AUGUST 24TH TO AUGUST 31ST

Prices rise 58% of the time during the fourth quarter of August. The average annual gain is +0.23%. The recent trend remains strong. Between 1984 and 1993, the fourth-quarter record is eight up and two down, one of the year's best quarterly records.

Analysis of daily price shifts shows a generally strong pattern of profitable days. The 24th has been especially good to investors in recent years. Since 1984, its record is six up and one down (*see Figure 9.4*).

Not a good time for long-term investments

If you are contemplating a purchase to take advantage of a good trading environment, be careful. Don't make any long-term investments. The impending arrival of risky September trading conditions means that, in some years, investors should begin closing out their open positions at the end of this quarter or during September's first quarter.

If you do decide to make a purchase in the fourth quarter, the best time to do it is if prices have risen steadily or fallen steadily in the preceding periods. There have been nine occasions since 1952 when prices rose in the first half of August by up to +3.56% *and* the third quarter. Fourth-quarter prices rose in seven of them.

Rose (7)

Fell (1)

Unchanged (1)

Fourth-quarter record after a price rise in August's first half by up to +3.56% and a rise in the third quarter (since 1952)

Figure 9.4

PERCENTAGE OF TIME PRICES RISE EACH TRADING DAY IN AUGUST'S FOURTH QUARTER

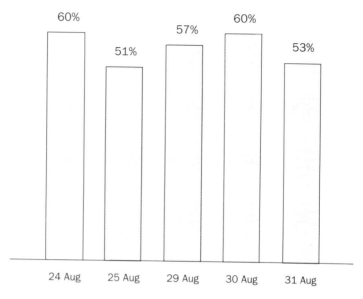

Figure 9.4: Prices rise on most days in this quarter. The 24th has been quite profitable since 1984 with a record of six ups and one down.

Likewise, if prices fall in the first half and the third quarter, the odds favour a fourth-quarter rise. There have been 11 occasions on record since 1939 where a decline occurred in the first half and third quarter. Fourth-quarter prices rose nine times.

Rose (9)

Fell (1)

Unchanged (1)

Fourth-quarter record after a price decline in August's first half and third quarter (since 1939)

CHAPTER TEN – SEPTEMBER 1995

> September investments are money-losing propositions. A £1,000 investment in 1919, placed in shares every September and in cash for the rest of each year, would have shrunk to £817 by 1993. September has a number of characteristics in common with May and June, in addition to losing money. All three are good to investors in most years but sporadic Big Hits affect the long-term average. Another key similarity: profits are good in the first quarter of each month. When troubles do occur, they often cluster in the second to fourth segments of the month.
>
> Despite the red ink, you can profit by following key price signals. Even better, the September trend has become an excellent tool with which to forecast the odds of profiting in October to December.

September is not a good month in which to own shares in the long-run. It is ranked a lowly tenth on monthly investment potential. Only May and June are worse. Between 1919 and 1993, September prices fell at a yearly average of -0.15%, equal to five points on a 3300 FT-SE 100 (*see Table 10.1*).

The month shares an important characteristic with May and June. In most years, the month is good to investors. But every so often, it gets slammed by the markets. The 'hit' is so severe that it hurts the average performance of the entire decade.

Higher income taxes

Take the 1930s as an example: the average share price dropped during this decade because of 1939 when prices fell by -12.13%. In that month, the market was buffeted by the declaration of war, news that Germany and Russia invaded Poland, the loss of 20 allied ships to U-boats and a War Budget which raised income tax to its highest-ever figure. The record for the rest of the decade was six up and three down, and an average annual increase of +0.94%.

The 1940s had no out-of-the-ordinary monthly decline. The September record was eight up and two down, and an average increase of +1.26%. The 1950s losing performance of -0.08% per year was caused by 1957's decline of -9.08%. The decline was in response to an increase in base rates to counter inflation.

Table 10.1

SEPTEMBER PRICE RISES AND DECLINES: 1919–1993

	Average September price change	Up	Down
1920–29	-1.01%	3	7
1930–39	-0.37%	6	4
1940–49	1.26%	8	2
1950–59	-0.08%	5	5
1960–69	0.87%	5	5
1970–79	-0.83%	6	4
1980–89	-1.03%	5	5
1990–93	-0.40%	1	3
Average September price change	-0.15%	40	35

Table 10.1: From 1930–1989, prices rose at least half the time each decade. September's problem is occasional Big Hits which ruin the performance record for the entire decade. One occurred in 1939, 1957, 1972, 1974, and 1981. There were no Big Hits in the profitable 1940s and '60s.

Rates rose to 7%. The rest of the decade saw five ups and four downs and an average increase of +0.92%.

The 1960s saw five up months, five down months, no unusual price action, and an average monthly price increase of +0.87%. The poor results of the 1970s was affected by 1972 (down -11.01%) and 1974 (down -12.35%). Inflation dominated September's economic news in both years. Here is one September 1974 headline: 'UK nurses get raises of up to 58%'. The rest of the decade saw six ups and two downs, and an average increase of +1.88%.

And in the latest complete decade, the Bull Market 1980s, poor results were due to a -16.94% decline in 1981. The record for the rest of the decade was five ups, four downs and an average increase of +0.74%.

Beware of the unexpected Big Hit

As you can see, September tends to be an 'okay' month most of the time – until it gets clobbered by a Big Hit. Note, however, that conditions are not uniform throughout the month. The first quarter is quite profitable in most years. The problems, when they occur, tend to cluster in the second, third, and fourth quarters (*see Figure 10.1*).

Figure 10.1

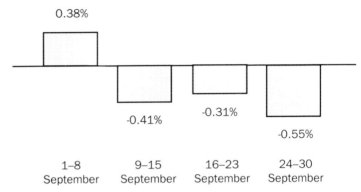

PROFITABILITY OF SEPTEMBER'S FOUR QUARTERS

0.38%

-0.41%

-0.31%

-0.55%

| 1–8 September | 9–15 September | 16–23 September | 24–30 September |

Figure 10.1: Long-term investors make money in the first quarter. The remaining three quarters are steady money-losers.

If you can't predict when a surprise event will occur, or when markets suddenly decide to take fright of events that have been unfolding over a long period of time, be warned that sudden, often unexpected, September price declines can wipe out years' worth of accumulated profits. But if you can figure out how to avoid the bad years, or at least some of them, there's money to be made in this month. Fortunately, there are a number of ways.

In last year's edition, we pointed out one winning strategy: hold no shares (or move into Puts) in years when January share prices drop. We have refined the strategy since then. Here is the up-to-date version of it.

Watch January shifts

Since 1937, there were 16 years when January prices dropped.[1] In 13 of those years, September prices also dropped. Five of the 13 were Big Hit years. The average September price decline during these 16 years was -3.95%, equal to 130 points on an FT-SE 100 in the area of 3300. And one of the three exceptions was a mere +0.20% increase in 1978. The last time the January Signal flashed was in 1993. September prices fell -2.59%, right in the middle of a very strong Bull Market run.

---

[1] Reminder: All monthly calculations are based on the FT-Non-Financial Index, formerly the FT-'500'; unless otherwise stated, they are based on data from 1919–1993. All daily, quarterly, and bi-monthly calculations are based on the Ordinary Share Index, also known as the FT-30; unless otherwise stated, they are based on data from 1935-1993.

Rose (3)

Fell (13)

September's record after a January fall (since 1937)

Historical trend analysis reveals several other trends that have done a good job of anticipating the direction of September price shifts.

12-month trend   If prices have fallen between -11.79% to -32.01% in the past twelve months, and the preceding three-month trend (June to August) is negative, September prices will probably rise. Out of 11 years which followed this scenario, September prices fell just once. This signal last flashed in 1992. After a -16.19% drop in the three months ending August 31st, September prices shot up by +9.01%, in response to our withdrawal from the ERM.

Rose (10)

Fell (1)

September's record after previous 12-month fall of -11.79% to -32.01% and a three-month fall

Six-month trend   If the preceding six-month trend has risen within a range of +15.04% to +24.67%, September prices will probably rise. Out of 11 years with a price rise of this magnitude in the run-up to September, September prices rose 10 times. The average increase during these 11 years was +2.42%, equal to 80 points on a 3300 FT-SE 100.

Rose (10)

Fell (1)

September's record after previous six month rise of +15.04% to +24.67%

FIRST QUARTER OF SEPTEMBER – SEPTEMBER 1ST TO SEPTEMBER 8TH

Although the month of September can be painful to investors, its first quarter is a consistent money-maker. Prices have risen in each of the five full decades on record. The average rate of increase is +0.38% per year. Prices rise in 61% of all Septembers (*see Table 10.2*).

Analysis of price trends on a day-by-day basis reveals a pattern of strength throughout the middle of the quarter. However, prices tend to disappoint on the first and last day of the quarter. Be especially cautious on September 8th. Since 1984, the record on this day has been one up and five down (*see Figure 10.2*).

Table 10.2

PERCENTAGE PRICE CHANGE SEPTEMBER: 1935–1993

	September 1–8	September 9–15	September 16–23	September 24–30
Average annual price change				
1935–39	-0.16%	-2.63%	-1.54%	0.67%
1940–49	0.11%	0.48%	0.12%	-0.08%
1950–59	0.06%	0.15%	-0.58%	-0.09%
1960–69	1.09%	-0.38%	0.50%	-0.77%
1970–79	0.87%	0.00%	-0.89%	-1.53%
1980–89	0.43%	-0.94%	-0.50%	-0.93%
1990–93	-0.63%	-1.07%	0.71%	-0.44%
Average quarterly price change	0.38%	-0.41%	-0.31%	-0.55%
Number of years in which prices:				
rose	36	24	29	26
fell	23	35	30	33

Table 10.2: The first-quarter investor made money in every full decade since the 1940s. The second- to fourth-quarter investor has been a steady money-loser in recent decades, including the Bull Market 1980s.

Figure 10.2   **PERCENTAGE OF TIME PRICES RISE EACH TRADING DAY IN SEPTEMBER'S FIRST QUARTER**

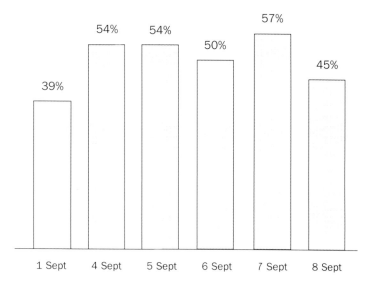

Figure 10.2: The weakest two days of the quarter are the first and last days. Be especially cautious on September 8. Prices have risen just once on this day since 1984.

The direction of first-quarter prices is frequently tipped off by the price trend for August. We first called attention to this in the *1994 Investor's Diary*. Here is an improved update. Since 1957, a shift of -4.74% to +4.69% in August is often followed by a price increase in September's first quarter. Out of 21 years with an August shift within this range, September's first quarter rose 19 times and generated an average profit of +1.27% per year. This signal last flashed in 1992 when first-quarter prices rose +1.79% after an August drop of -3.77%.

Rose (19)

Fell (2)

First-quarter record after an August shift of -4.74% to +4.81% (since 1960)

145

Since 1960, if prices shift in the fourth quarter of August within a range of -0.66% to +1.19%, shares usually rise in value during September's first quarter. Out of 14 years with a shift within the defined range, first-quarter prices rose 12 times.

Rose (12)

Fell (2)

First-quarter record after an August fourth-quarter shift of -0.66% to +1.19% (since 1960)

SECOND QUARTER OF SEPTEMBER – SEPTEMBER 9TH TO SEPTEMBER 15TH

As a general rule, do not buy any shares in the second quarter of September. Not only are the odds of making a profit against you, but the third and fourth quarters of the month are also generally money-losers. If you are thinking of selling shares you already own, the odds favour doing it at the beginning of the quarter.

Prices tend to fall this quarter

The average share price drops -0.41% each year during this quarter. Prices have risen in just 24 of the last 59 years (41%). Even during the 1980s' Bull Market decade the record was four up, six down and an average decrease of -0.94%. Thus far into the 1990s, prices have fallen in three out of four years (*see Table 10.3*).

Analysis of daily price trends confirms this general pattern of weakness (*see Figure 10.3*). The only steadily-profitable day in the quarter is the 14th. In 1995, you should be especially cautious on the first and last day of the quarter.

▶ When the second Monday of September lands on the 10th –12th, share prices often fall. Since 1935, second Monday prices rose in just six out of 25 times (24%). In 1995, the 11th lands on a Monday.

▶ Since 1974, prices have risen on the 15th of the month in just three out of 14 years.

Table 10.3

PERCENTAGE PRICE CHANGE FOR SEPTEMBER SINCE 1980

	September 1–8	September 9–15	September 16–23	September 24–30
1980	1.67%	1.77%	-3.12%	-0.85%
1981	-3.92%	-3.08%	-7.39%	-3.92%
1982	2.60%	-1.94%	0.17%	0.16%
1983	0.88%	-2.34%	1.43%	-0.61%
1984	-0.23%	0.90%	1.40%	-0.34%
1985	0.68%	-0.87%	-1.64%	0.41%
1986	0.90%	-2.58%	-1.37%	-3.53%
1987	0.88%	0.01%	3.82%	0.57%
1988	-0.50%	1.40%	1.74%	2.05%
1989	1.32%	-2.70%	-0.01%	-3.27%
1990	-3.25%	-1.76%	-4.49%	-0.10%
1991	0.69%	-1.23%	-2.48%	0.25%
1992	1.79%	0.88%	10.20%	-2.17%
1993	-1.72%	-2.17%	-0.38%	0.26%
Average quarterly price change				
1980–89	0.43%	-0.94%	-0.50%	-0.93%
1980–93	0.13%	-0.98%	-0.15%	-0.79%
Number of years in which prices:				
rose	9	5	6	6
fell	5	9	8	8

Table 10.3: From 1980 to the present, the second to fourth quarters of September performed poorly. The third quarter is especially worthy of note. The average stayed in negative territory despite 1992's whopping +10.20% rise in prices in response to our withdrawal from the ERM.

The January rule helps forecast September's declines

The only way to make money consistently in the second quarter is to bet against the market. To help you improve the odds of identifying periods when prices will decline, the market sends several useful signals.

One of them is the January rule which does such a good job of anticipating September's monthly declines. If you are toying

Figure 10.3

PERCENTAGE OF TIME PRICES RISE EACH TRADING DAY IN SEPTEMBER'S SECOND QUARTER

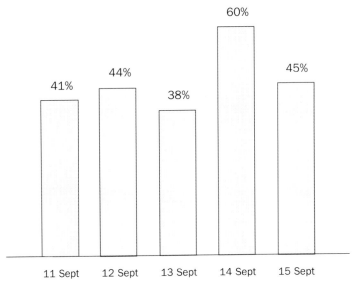

Figure 10.3: The 14th is steadily profitable, the only good day in the quarter. Prices are especially likely to fall when September 11 lands on a Monday, as will happen in 1995. Prices have risen on September 15 just three times since 1974.

with the idea of buying Puts, your short-term profit potential will improve if you buy them in years that January's prices declined by up to -7.57%. Out of 15 years in which January prices declined by up to -7.57%, September second-quarter prices fell 13 times (87%). The average price loss was -1.25%.

Rose (2)

Fell (13)

Second-quarter record after a January fall of up to -7.57%

Profit on the down-side

A second signal which improves your odds of profiting on the down-side is the direction of prices in the preceding few quarters. If they shift in the fourth quarter of August by -2.29% to +0.52% *and* rise in the first quarter of September, the odds are especially good they will fall in the second quarter. Out of 12 occasions since 1957 when the price of the average share shifted in the preceding periods within the appropriate range, second-quarter prices declined 11 times (92%). The average quarterly decline during those 12 years was -1.47%.

Rose (1)

Fell (11)

Second-quarter record after an August fourth-quarter shift of -2.29% to +0.52% and September first-quarter rise (since 1957)

THIRD QUARTER OF SEPTEMBER – SEPTEMBER 16TH TO SEPTEMBER 23RD

As in the second quarter, investors usually lose money by investing during the third quarter. Between 1935 and 1993, the third quarter of September rose 49% of the time and generated an average loss of -0.31% per year.

A review of recent price trends reveals that the average share price fell in both the 1970s and '80s. So far in the '90s, the record is three out of four declines. But the single exception, a +10.20% increase in prices in 1992 in response to Britain's withdrawal from the ERM, will exert a strong influence on this decade's average performance and disguise the period's poor results among lazy investors who merely look at the overall average.

The January trend
If you wish to bet on the down-side, here are two signals to increase your chance of success. Since 1952, a January decline of up to -7.57% correlates with a poor third-quarter per-formance. Third-quarter prices declined in nine of 11 years in which January prices fell by this amount. The average decline was -2.24%.

Rose (2)

Fell (9)

Third-quarter record after a January decline of up to -7.57% (since 1952)

Figure 10.4   **PERCENTAGE OF TIME PRICES RISE EACH TRADING DAY IN SEPTEMBER'S THIRD QUARTER**

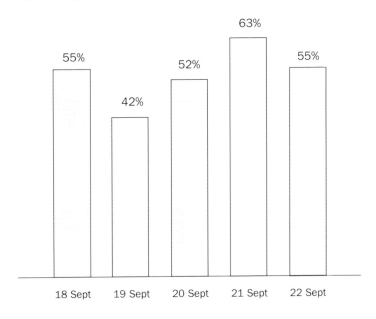

Figure 10.4: Be careful. The 19th, 20th, and 22nd are among the most volatile days of the month with an above-average likelihood of price shifts (up or down) in excess of 1%.

Watch prices in first half

A second useful signal is the direction of prices in the first half of September. If they fall in both the first and second quarter, with a second-quarter decline of no more than -3.08%, the odds of a third-quarter decline increase. Since 1946, there have been 12 occasions when first-half prices fell within the designated range. In 10 of those years, the fall was immediately followed by a third-quarter decline.

Rose (2) ☐

Fell (10) ☐

Third-quarter record after a first-quarter fall (any amount) and second-quarter fall of up to -3.08% (since 1946)

On the up-side, if the first-half price trend rises, so will the third quarter. Since 1958, share prices rose +0.61% to +3.45% in the first half in 11 different years. Third-quarter prices rose each time.

Rose (11)

Fell (0)

Third-quarter record after a first-half price rise of +0.61% to +3.45% (since 1958)

FOURTH QUARTER OF SEPTEMBER – SEPTEMBER 24TH TO SEPTEMBER 30TH

The fourth quarter of September offers very poor investment potential. It is the third-worst quarter of the entire year. Investors lose -0.55%, on average, each year they invest in this quarter.

Between 1935 and 1993, prices rose in the fourth quarter only 44% of the time. Investors lost money in every single decade on record. September 26th is the worst trading day of the entire year. Prices rise just 22% of the time on this date (*see Table 10.4*).

Table 10.4   **THE WORST DAYS OF THE YEAR**

	Percent of time prices rise
September 26	22%
October 9	26%
September 23	28%
February 21	29%
November 22	31%
October 10	32%
February 4 & March 11 (tied)	33%
February 12	34%
September 10 & 16 (tied)	35%

Table 10.4: Four of the 11 worst days of the year are in September.

Figure 10.5

PERCENTAGE OF TIME PRICES RISE EACH TRADING DAY IN SEPTEMBER'S FOURTH QUARTER

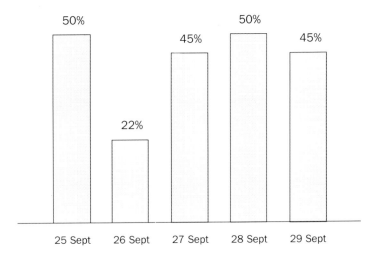

Figure 10.5: The 26th is the worst day of the entire year. The 25th, 27th, and 29th tend to be very volatile with an above-average likelihood of big (1% or more) price swings.

For down-side investors, we find two correlations that are associated with an increased likelihood of a fourth-quarter fall.

Look to January for a pointer

Once again, January prices strongly correlate with a poor September performance. Prices in the fourth quarter declined in 10 of the 11 years in which January prices fell by -1.23% to -7.57%. The average decline was -1.68%.

Rose (1)

Fell (10)

Fourth-quarter record after a January decline of -1.23% to -7.57%

Here is a second down-side signal to which we first called attention in the *1994 Investor's Diary*. If prices fall in September's first, second and third quarters, they are especially likely to fall in the fourth quarter. Since 1935, there have been 11 years in which prices fell in each of the three preceding quarters. They fell in the fourth quarter in nine of those years. One of the two exceptions, in 1993, saw a price rise of just +0.26% after three consecutive quarterly declines.

Rose (2) □

Fell (9) ▭

Fourth-quarter record after prices drop in all three September quarters

SEPTEMBER PRICE TREND PREDICTS THE DIRECTION OF PRICES FOR THE REST OF THE YEAR

It's not widely known, but September is an excellent contrarian predictor of fourth-quarter price trends. Since 1959, a price drop in September is usually followed with price increases in the final three months of the year.

Let's start by putting things into perspective. From 1959 to 1993, fourth-quarter prices rose 71% of the time. Share prices increased at an average of +2.73% per year.

Pin-point when shares rise

During this period, there were 15 years when September prices fell by -0.67% or more. Shares rose in the next three months in 14 of those years (93%) at an average rate of +7.36%. The sole exception occurred in 1974 at the tail end of a vicious two-year-long Bear Market when the October to December period dropped -13.07% after a September drop of -12.35%.

Rose (14) ▭

Fell (1) □

October to December record after a September decline of at least -0.67% (since 1959)

During the other 20 years of this period, when September prices either fell slightly or rose by any amount, the record for the last three months of the year was 11 up and nine down, with an average loss of -0.75%.

CHAPTER ELEVEN – OCTOBER 1995

GED

Bull Market bashes end with
October crashes

Forget the rhyme: 'Bull Market bashes end with October crashes.' October is profitable over the long-run. But most of the profits are generated in the first quarter of the month. The trend soon weakens. Prices are especially likely to fall in the fourth quarter. Its record over the past 20 years is five up and 15 down, the year's worst performance.

Mention October to the average investor and the losses of 1929 or 1987 immediately come to mind.

Despite the negative connotation, October investors do pretty well over the long-run. Between 1919, when records first began, and 1993, October prices rose 61% of the time (*see Table 11.1*).

October investors lost a small amount of money in the 1920s. The source of the problem was not 1929 as many would guess but 1921 when share prices fell by -9.76%.[1]

---

[1] Reminder: All monthly calculations are based on the FT-Non-Financial Index, formerly the FT-'500'; unless otherwise stated, they are based on data from 1919–1993. All daily, quarterly, and bi-monthly calculations are based on the Ordinary Share Index, also known as the FT-30; unless otherwise stated, they are based on data from 1935-1993.

Table 11.1

OCTOBER PRICE RISES AND DECLINES: 1919–1993

	Average October price change	Up	Down/ no change
1920–29	-0.11%	6	4
1930–39	3.58%	7	3
1940–49	0.78%	6	4
1950–59	2.87%	7	3
1960–69	1.05%	6	4
1970–79	-0.93%	4	6
1980–89	-0.97%	7	3
1990–93	2.01%	3	1
Average October price change	0.89%	46	29

Table 11.1: October was steadily profitable in the 1930s to '60s. Investors may not have profited every single year but did quite well over the long-run. The apparent losses in the 1970s and '80s were due to a single year in each decade: a loss of -10.12% in 1976 and -26.21% in 1987. The average annual return in the rest of each decade was positive.

October 1929

Prices rose in six of the other nine years of the 1920s, and produced an average annual profit even with 1929's performance included. Incidentally, October's prices fell by just -5.46% in 1929, much less than many modern day investors would guess. It is what happened in the years following that gives 1929 its notoriety.

Despite the Great Depression and the price weakness in the run-up to World War II, October investors made an average annual profit of +3.58% in the 1930s when it was the Number One-ranked month. The month continued to be profitable in the 1940s through to the 1960s.

Recent performance OK

The trend appears to have weakened in the recent past with average annual losses recorded in the 1970s and 1980s. But in each decade, one year accounted for the poor results: 1976 (down -10.12%) and 1987 (down -26.21%). The average annual return was positive in the remainder of both decades.

Even with 1921, 1976, and 1987 included in computations, the 75-year average October price rise is +0.89%, equal to 29 points on an FT-SE 100 in the area of 3300. Historically,

October is the fifth-best month in which to invest in shares. A hypothetical investor who invested only in October, from 1919 to 1993, and switched to cash for the rest of the year, would have run up his £1,000 to £1,701.

If you are planning to purchase shares to catch the October up-turn, be sure to do so at the beginning of the month as the first quarter is, by far, the most profitable (*see Figure 11.1*). Prices often drop in the rest of the month. The fourth-quarter's performance has been especially poor recently. Prices fell in 15 of the last 20 years, the worst performance of the entire year.

Investors can increase October profits by identifying specific years when prices are especially likely to rise. Short sellers or Put buyers can also profit by identifying years with a high likelihood of October price drops. There are several historical trends which have done a good job of anticipating the direction of October price shifts.

The direction that prices have shifted in the past 12 months is a good October price signal. There have been 13 years in which prices rose in the past 12 months by +13.54% to +20.62%. October share prices rose in 12 of those years. The sole exception was in 1983 when prices fell by -1.79%. The average annual increase during these 13 years is +3.15% which is equal to 104 points on an FT-SE 100 in the area of 3300.

Rose (12)

Fell (1)

October record after a price rise of +13.54% to +20.62% in past 12 months

In the *1994 Investor's Diary*, we advised investors to increase the odds of making a profitable October investment by watching the price trend in August and September. Here is an improved update. Since 1956, there were 10 years when shares moved up or down by less than 4.00% in August and by +1.22% to -9.08% in September. October prices fell all 10 times.

Figure 11.1

PROFITABILITY OF OCTOBER'S FOUR QUARTERS

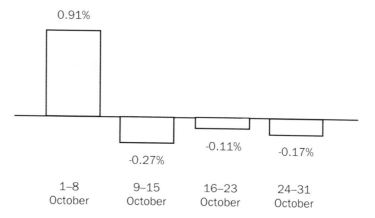

Figure 11.1: The first quarter is the biggest profit-maker in most years. The trend soon deteriorates. The second quarter is worst over the long-run but the fourth-quarter record in the last 20 years is simply horrible – 15 declines out of 20, the worst performance of all 48 quarters.

Rose (0)

Fell (10)

October record after an August price shift of less than 4.00% (up or down) and a September price shift of +1.22% to -9.08% (since 1956)

Since 1952, if August prices rise by at least 4.00%, and are followed by a September price increase under 5.00%, or a September fall of any amount, October prices tend to rise. Since 1952, there were 15 years with August and September price shifts in the correct range. October prices rose each time, at a whopping average annual rate of +4.54%.

Rose (15)

Fell (0)

October record after an August price rise of at least +4.00% and a September rise of less than +5.00% or a September fall (since 1952)

Here is a final August/September trend to watch: There have been 17 years when prices rose in the preceding two months by +3.19% to +5.88%. October prices rose in 15 of those years. The two exceptions were back in 1949 and 1969. The average annual increase in prices during these 17 years was +2.06%.

Rose (15)

Fell (2)

October record after an August/September price rise of +3.19% to +5.88%

FIRST QUARTER OF OCTOBER – OCTOBER 1ST TO OCTOBER 8TH

As for other months, there are widely different profit potentials associated with investments made during different segments of October.

The best segment of the month, by far, is the first quarter. It has risen 64% of the time and produced an average annual profit in every single decade on record. Between 1935 and 1993, the average first-quarter profit was +0.91% per year, third-best quarter for the entire year (*see Table 11.2*).

If you are planning to buy shares during October, past performance suggests that the best time to do it is at the very beginning of the month to take advantage of the anticipated price rise. You will not profit every single year, but in the long-run, the odds favour this investment strategy. Thinking of selling? The odds suggest you will benefit by waiting a few more days.

October 2nd
is best

Analysis of price trends on a day-by-day basis finds the most profitable point of the quarter to be at the very beginning. Prices rise 62% of the time on October 2nd (*see Figure 11.2*). The trend then drifts downward. Unfortunately, the first Monday of the month is often a money-loser and October 2nd falls on a Monday in 1995 (*see Table 11.3*).

Although a +0.91% average quarterly profit is nothing to complain about, you can out-perform the averages by watching the direction of prices in September's fourth quarter. Since

Table 11.2

PERCENTAGE PRICE CHANGE OCTOBER: 1935–1993

	October 1–8	October 9–15	October 16–23	October 24–31
Average annual price change				
1935–39	0.46%	0.24%	1.56%	0.47%
1940–49	0.70%	-0.74%	0.42%	0.76%
1950–59	0.31%	1.10%	0.65%	-0.42%
1960–69	0.86%	-0.31%	-1.45%	1.26%
1970–79	1.25%	-0.72%	0.08%	-2.27%
1980–89	0.83%	-0.36%	-2.20%	-0.02%
1990–93	2.97%	-1.70%	2.69%	-1.33%
Average quarterly price change	0.91%	-0.27%	-0.11%	-0.17%
Number of years in which prices:				
rose	38	27	31	26
fell	21	32	26	32
remained unchanged	–	–	2	1

Table 11.2: The poor record of the second and fourth quarters is more than a short-term run of poor luck. For both quarters, prices fall in most years. In contrast, the third quarter has been performing better than the averages suggest. Without 1987's third-quarter decline of -22.95%, the 1980–89 third-quarter average would be +0.10%, and the overall third-quarter average would be +0.25%.

1949, if fourth-quarter prices fell by -1.50% to -5.66%, the odds of a rise in October's first quarter was quite high. Out of 16 years with a fourth-quarter fall of this magnitude, first-quarter prices rose 14 times (88%). The average price rise was +1.46% in those 16 years.

Rose (14)

Fell (2)

First-quarter record after a September fourth-quarter price decline of -1.50% to -5.66% (since 1949)

Figure 11.2   **PERCENTAGE OF TIME PRICES RISE EACH TRADING DAY IN OCTOBER'S FIRST QUARTER**

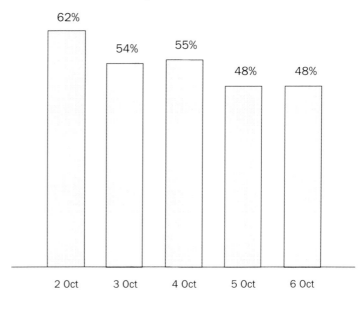

Figure 11.2: The best day of the quarter is October 2. Unfortunately, the odds of an October 2 profit are lower than average in 1995 because it lands on a Monday.

Prices also tend to rise in years with a September second-half up-move. We first called attention to this trend in the *1994 Investor's Diary*. Here's an improved update. Since 1947, there have been 17 years in which September's third-quarter prices either fell by no more than -1.64% or rose, and fourth-quarter prices rose by any amount. Prices continued to rise in October's first quarter in 15 of those years (88%). The average price rise was +1.64% in those 17 years. The two exceptions to the rule occurred in 1964 and 1965.

Rose (15)   [   ]

Fell (2)   [ ]

First-quarter record after a September third-quarter price decline of -1.64% or less, or a rise, and a fourth-quarter rise (since 1947)

Table 11.3   **PERCENTAGE OF TIME PRICES RISE ON 1–4 OCTOBER: 1935–1993**

	Prices rise
Total	57%
Monday	39%
Rest of week	61%

Table 11.3: The first Monday in October is not good for investors.

SECOND QUARTER OF OCTOBER – OCTOBER 9TH TO OCTOBER 15TH

Second-quarter prices rose just 46% of the time between 1935 and 1993, much less often than the first quarter. Prices fell -0.27% on average, making the second quarter of October the worst performer of the month over the long-run.

The last profitable time period for the second quarter was in the 1950s. The second-quarter investor lost money in the 1940s, '60s, '70s and '80s. Since 1987, second-quarter prices fell in six of seven years (*see Table 11.4*).

Red ink in abundance

Analysis of price trends on a day-by-day basis reveals lots of red ink. October 9th is the worst day of the month and second-worst of the entire year. Prices rise just 26% of the time. October 10th is not much better with price increases in just 32% of all years, second-worst day of the month and sixth-worst in the year. These two days, back-to-back, are the worst two-day stretch of the entire year (*see Figure 11.3*). Unfortunately, there is even more bad news. October 9th and 10th seem to do especially poorly when they land on a Monday or Tuesday (*see Table 11.5*). In 1995, October 9th lands on a Monday and October 10th lands on a Tuesday.

Bet against the market

In the long-run, it pays to stand aside or bet against the market during this stretch of the month. This is especially true in 1995. We find no signal that tips off a consistent and reasonably-sized profit opportunity on the up-side.

For readers interested in a short-term bet against the market, one very powerful signal exists. Unfortunately it flashes infrequently. But when it does flash, the chance of falling second-quarter prices is very high.

Table 11.4

PERCENTAGE PRICE CHANGE DURING OCTOBER SINCE 1980

	October 1–8	October 9–15	October 16–23	October 24–31
1980	-0.31%	1.25%	1.44%	-1.22%
1981	2.59%	-2.97%	-2.39%	1.43%
1982	2.56%	1.86%	2.57%	-3.34%
1983	1.02%	-4.41%	1.67%	1.93%
1984	-0.21%	1.73%	-1.63%	2.40%
1985	0.78%	1.66%	2.68%	1.69%
1986	1.72%	2.27%	-2.08%	2.84%
1987	0.71%	-2.89%	-22.95%	-2.57%
1988	0.94%	0.24%	1.02%	-0.50%
1989	-1.48%	-2.30%	-2.34%	-2.89%
1990	11.07%	-4.60%	1.69%	-3.73%
1991	-1.48%	-0.91%	-0.37%	-0.19%
1992	0.53%	-1.08%	7.11%	-0.90%
1993	1.76%	-0.20%	2.34%	-0.48%
Average quarterly price change				
1980–89	0.83%	-0.36%	-2.20%	-0.02%
1980–93	1.44%	-0.74%	-0.80%	-0.40%
Number of years in which prices:				
rose	10	6	8	5
fell	4	8	6	9

Table 11.4: The relative strength of the first quarter continued into the 1980s and '90s. The second and fourth quarters have been quite weak since 1987.

Table 11.5

PERCENTAGE OF TIME PRICES RISE ON 9–10 OCTOBER: 1935–1993

	Prices rise
Total	29%
Monday, Tuesday, or Friday	16%
Rest of week	47%

Table 11.5: It's generally hard to make a profit on October 9 and 10. The odds are even lower if these days land on a Monday or Tuesday as they do in 1995.

Figure 11.3

PERCENTAGE OF TIME PRICES RISE EACH TRADING DAY IN OCTOBER'S SECOND QUARTER

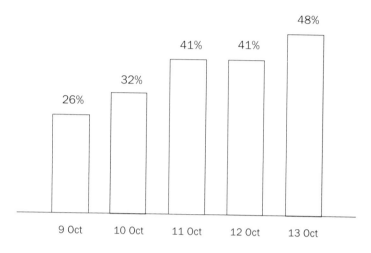

Figure 11.3: October 9 is the second worst day of the entire year. The rest of the quarter is not very good either. October 9 and 10 comprise the worst two-day stretch of the year.

If prices decline in September's first half, second half, and October's first quarter, they are almost certain to decline in the second quarter. Since 1935, there have been seven years in which prices fell in all three periods. The price fall continued through October's second quarter each time. The average price drop was -1.13%.

Rose (0) |

Fell (7) [   ]

Second-quarter record after a decline in September's first half, second half, and October's first quarter

If first-quarter prices shift within a tiny range of -0.18% to +0.71%, second-quarter prices are likely to fall. Out of 10 shifts within this range, second-quarter prices fell nine times.

Rose (1)

Fell (9)

Second-quarter record after a first-quarter shift of -0.18% to +0.71%

And if prices fall during the preceding five days, October 9th and 10th are extremely likely to fall. Out of 36 times with a price decline in the previous five trading days, October 9th and 10th each rose just once.

Rose (2)

Fell (32)

No change (2)

Trend on October 9-10 if prices fell in preceding five trading days

Third Quarter of October – October 16th to October 23rd

At first glance, the third quarter is not a particularly good time to be in the stock market for long-term investors. Since 1935, it has been averaging an annual loss of -0.11%.

But a closer look reveals some good news. Prices rose 31 times (53%), fell 26 times and were unchanged in two years. The average annual loss is caused by the 1987 crash, which occurred in this quarter, when prices dropped -22.95%. If 1987 were eliminated, a small profit was produced in the remaining 58 years, of +0.29% per year.

Don't be too quick to buy shares

Analysis of price trends on a day-by-day basis finds the weakest prices at the very beginning of the quarter (*see Figure 11.4*). The price trend improves for the next four days. But don't be too quick to buy shares. The quarter to follow is one of the year's worst. For this reason, the best advice for long-term investors contemplating a purchase of shares is to wait for the next few weeks to pass. But for short-term traders, there are

Figure 11.4

PERCENTAGE OF TIME PRICES RISE EACH TRADING DAY IN OCTOBER'S THIRD QUARTER

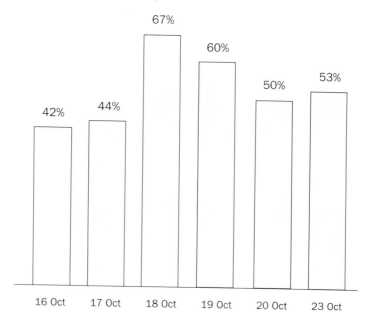

Figure 11.4: The odds of making a profit are above-average once the first two days of the quarter have passed. October 18 is the best day of the month.

good opportunities to profit in this quarter by watching the price trend in the first half of October.

Since 1964, there were 10 years when prices dropped in October's first half by no more than -2.49%. They continued to decline in the third quarter in nine of these years.

Rose (1)

Fell (9)

Third-quarter record after a first-half price decline of up to -2.49% (since 1964)

There were another 14 years when prices rose in October's first half between +1.55% to +4.02%. They continued to rise in the third quarter in 12 of those years (86%).

Rose (12)

Fell (2)

Third-quarter record after a first-half price rise of +1.55% to +4.02%

Another first-half trend

If prices rise in both the first and second quarters of the month, third-quarter prices are even more likely to rise. Since 1942, there have been 14 years in which prices rose in the first quarter by no more than +4.96% and in the second quarter by any amount. Third-quarter prices also increased in 12 of those years (86%), at an average annual rate of +1.10%.

Rose (12)

Fell (2)

Third-quarter record after a first-quarter price rise of up to +4.96% and a second-quarter rise of any amount (since 1942)

And if prices rise three quarters in a row – the last quarter of September, first quarter of October and the second quarter – third-quarter prices are especially likely to rise. Since 1942, there have been eight years with price rises in three consecutive quarters. Third-quarter prices rose in seven of those years, at an average annual rate of +1.63%. The single exception occurred back in 1958.

Rose (7)

Fell (1)

Third-quarter record after a first-, second- and third-quarter price rise (since 1942)

FOURTH QUARTER OF OCTOBER – OCTOBER 24TH TO OCTOBER 31ST

The fourth quarter of October is a poor time to be holding shares. Prices decline at an average annual rate of -0.17%. Between 1935–1993, the record was 26 up (44%), 32 down and one no change.

In the last 20 years, from 1974 to 1993, the fourth-quarter record has been atrocious. Prices have fallen 15 times, the worst record of the entire year (*see Table 11.6*). Since the 1987 crash, fourth-quarter prices have fallen six times in a row, tied with one other as the worst performance of the year.

The odds favour a price drop

As a general rule of thumb, the odds favour a price decline in this quarter. It's not a good time to move into the market unless you are betting on the down-side.

If you do bet on a price drop, the chance of a successful bet improves if prices rise weakly in the first half of October. Since 1964, there have been 14 occasions where prices rose by no more than +1.19% in the first half or fell, and rose no more than +1.44% or fell in the third quarter. Fourth-quarter prices continued to drop in 12 of them (86%). The average yearly decline was -1.43%.

Rose (2)

Fell (12)

Fourth-quarter record after a first-half price rise of no more than +1.19 or a fall, and a third-quarter rise of no more than +1.44% or a fall (since 1964)

Another signal to watch is the direction of prices in the third quarter by itself. Since 1947, third-quarter prices have risen +1.02% to +2.63% in 12 years. Fourth-quarter prices fell in 10 of those years (83%).

Rose (2)

Fell (10)

Fourth-quarter record after a third-quarter price rise of +1.02% to +2.63% (since 1947)

167

Figure 11.5   **PERCENTAGE OF TIME PRICES RISE EACH TRADING DAY IN OCTOBER'S FOURTH QUARTER**

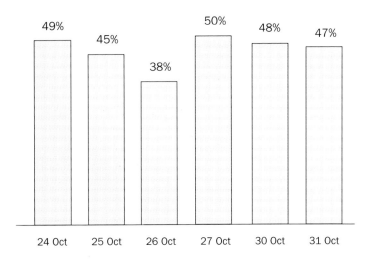

Figure 11.5: Prices rise less than half the time on most days in this quarter.

Table 11.6   **YEAR'S SIX BEST AND SIX WORST QUARTERS IN LAST 20 YEARS: 1974–1993**

Best	Number of increases	Worst	Number of increases
January 4th quarter	17	October 4th quarter	5
April 2nd quarter	16	March 3rd quarter	7
April 4th quarter	16	May 3rd quarter	7
March 1st quarter	15	June 2nd quarter	7
June 1st quarter	15	June 3rd quarter	7
December 4th quarter	15	Several at this level	8

Table 11.6: October's fourth quarter has become the year's worst performer, falling in 15 of the last 20 years.

CHAPTER TWELVE – NOVEMBER 1995

In historical terms, November is a poor month. It is ranked ninth in terms of monthly profitability. But the switch to a late autumn Budget Day changes everything. November price trends will probably improve just as March and April prices were strong when Budget Day was a spring-time event.

There are several important price trends surrounding Budget Day such as the high likelihood of a price drop in the week preceding Budget Day and a price rise on Budget Day itself. Even more important, the price trend in the four weeks preceding Budget Day often tips off where prices are heading in the four weeks to follow.

Between 1919 and 1993, November prices rose 59% of the time, fifth-best of all 12 months. Unfortunately, in profitable years, the average price increase was smaller than normal, and in money-losing years, the average decline was larger than normal. As a result, the average price rise over the 75 years studied was just +0.07% per year, much less than the risk-free return provided by a neighbourhood building society (*see Table 12.1*). A November investment, started in 1919 with £1,000, with money moved into cash for the other 11 months each year, would be worth just £969 in 1993. The first and second quarters produced most of the month's profits. The second half loses money in most years (*see Figure 12.1*).

The trend will change

This pattern of profit may now change because of the shift to a new, late autumn unified Budget Day in 1993. The effect of Budget Day on share prices is often quite significant, both in the run-up as well as the weeks that follow. When spring budgets began to occur in mid-April, in the 1940s, April's profits skyrocketed into the Number One-ranked position. When Budget Day was advanced still further into mid-March, March profits similarly rose.

With this latest Budget Day shift, we suspect that the long-term November trend will change. The change will probably affect share prices on Budget Day itself, as well as in the several weeks on either side of it.

Table 12.1

NOVEMBER PRICE RISES AND DECLINES: 1919–1993

	Average November price change	Up	Down
1920–29	-0.87%	4	6
1930–39	-0.98%	5	5
1940–49	2.90%	8	2
1950–59	-1.38%	5	5
1960–69	1.35%	7	3
1970–79	-2.39%	5	5
1980–89	1.85%	8	2
1990–93	-0.56%	2	2
Average November price change	0.07%	44	31

Table 12.1: November is the fifth-best month in terms of the number of times prices have risen, but only ninth-best in terms of the size of the increase. Over time, investors would have made more profit with their money in a risk-free building society savings account.

Budget Day

Do not be disheartened by the fear and gloom that seems to play so important a role in most pre-budget press coverage. Negative news is what sells so negative news is what gets delivered to the public. Regardless of the headlines, investors usually do well on Budget Day. Since 1936, share prices rose 71% of the time on Budget Day, held steady for 5% of the time and fell just 24% of the time. When prices do rise, the average increase is +0.95%. When prices fall, the average decrease is -0.68%.[1]

Budget Day gyrations are getting bigger. Since 1970, the average up-move is +1.42% and the average down-move -0.94%. Notice, though, the difference between the two averages is proportionately about the same as before.

---

[1] Reminder: All monthly calculations are based on the FT-Non-Financial Index, formerly the FT-'500'; unless otherwise stated, they are based on data from 1919–1993. All daily, quarterly, and bi-monthly calculations are based on the Ordinary Share Index, also known as the FT-30; unless otherwise stated, they are based on data from 1935-1993.

Figure 12.1

PROFITABILITY OF NOVEMBER'S FOUR QUARTERS

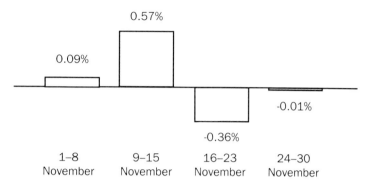

Figure 12.1: Over time, most November profits occur in the first half of the month, especially the second quarter.

Occasionally, the Chancellor's speech catches the stock market by surprise and prices react in a big way. In 1971, share prices rose by over 6% in response to the first Tory budget since 1964 as Chancellor Antony Barber reduced taxes and announced the eventual introduction of VAT. But in most years, key budget elements are tipped or leaked in advance, reducing the odds of the stock market being caught by surprise, and Budget Day shifts tend to be smaller.

If prices fall on Budget Day, watch out for further declines

When prices do fall on Budget Day, the problem is not just a single day's fall. It's what follows that should concern investors. History shows that if share prices do drop on Budget Day, the odds favour a further decline during the rest of budget week. Since 1938, there have been 10 occasions when share prices fell by at least -0.26% on Budget Day. Prices declined still further over the next three days in each of those years.

Rose (0)

Fell (10)

Trend of three days following Budget Day if Budget Day prices fall -0.26% or more

In most instances, the low point for the week was not even reached until Friday, although a few declines ended on Wednesday or Thursday. At their lowest point, prices were down by an average of -2.61% from their already depressed Budget Day low. That's a whopping 86 points on an FT-SE 100 in the area of 3300.

The run-up to Budget Day

For readers thinking of jumping the gun by purchasing shares in advance to catch the expected Budget Day up-move, don't do it. The odds are against making a profit. In the five pre-budget trading days, prices rise just 29% of the time and fall 71%. Regardless of how this year turns out, it's clear that nervous investors often use the run-up to Budget Day to dump shares.

Fortunately, the size and direction of all price shifts in the five pre-budget days often tips off which way Budget Day prices will shift. If prices manage to rise in the week before Budget Day, the odds heavily favour a Budget Day price rise. Out of 19 years with a price rise in the five-day run-up to Budget Day, Budget Day prices fell just twice on the big day.

Rose (17)

Fell (2)

Budget Day trend if prices rise in preceding five days

Similarly, if prices fall by 3% or more in the five-day run-up, there is a very strong chance they will also rise on Budget Day. Out of seven occasions with a decline of 3% or more, Budget Day prices rose in six of those years.

Rose (6)

Fell (1)

Budget Day trend if prices drop -3% or more in preceding five days

The weeks to follow

The Big Question is not what happens on Budget Day but what the Budget Day shifts tell us about future price trends. The direction of prices on Budget Day itself sends no usable signal to longer-term investors. Shares rise about the same amount of time in the four weeks that follow Budget Day in years with an up-move or down-move on Budget Day itself. So don't try to make a snap prediction of where prices are heading after noting Tuesday night's closing prices. Knee-jerk reactions by stock market gun-slingers are not reliable predictors of where prices are headed.

Watch prices in the run-up to Budget Day

There is a much better approach. The secret is to watch the price trend in the four week run-up to Budget Day. If prices rise by +6% or more, it is a very clear signal that further price increases are due in the four weeks that follow Budget Day. Good news is also signalled by a sharp decline in pre-four week price trend. If prices decline by at least 7%, they are also extremely likely to rise in the four weeks that follow as investors who avoided shares in anticipation of bad budget news, begin to bargain hunt.

There have been 11 moves in the four-week run-up to Budget Day of at least +6% on the up-side or -7% on the down-side. Four weeks later, prices were higher in every one of those years.

Rose (11)

Fell (0)

Trend in four weeks that follow Budget Day if prices rise +6% or more, or drop -7% or more in preceding four weeks

Be aware of direction *and* size of price moves following Budget Day

Another trend to watch is the direction of prices in the three days that follow Budget Day. It is during this period that the stock market seems to sort out the implications of the Chancellor's speech and its effect on the economy. If prices shift moderately on the Wednesday to Friday that follow Budget Day, they will probably continue to rise in the three weeks that follow. Be sure to watch the size of the price move, not just the direction.

If prices rise moderately in the first three post-budget trading days, within a range of +1.4% to +2.6%, there is a very high likelihood that they will rise still further in the next three weeks. In eight out of nine years with share price increases in

173

this range, they rose still higher three weeks later. The single exception was in October, 1945 in the midst of a national dock strike.

Rose (8)

Fell (1)

Trend in three weeks that follow Budget Day if prices rise +1.4% to +2.6% in three days that follow Budget Day

In 22 other years that saw sharper or weaker three-day price rises, the record three weeks later was 10 up and 12 down.

This kind of data doesn't definitely say what will happen this year, but it sends an important message for the long-run. If the three-day rise is too big or too small, the next three weeks are, on average, a losing proposition.

The same is true on the down-side. A medium-sized down-move in the three days following Budget Day is often associated with a solid up-move in the three weeks that follow. There have been 12 occasions with three-day falls between -1.47% and -3.02%. Prices rose in 11 of those years over the next three weeks.

Rose (11)

Fell (1)

Trend in three weeks that follow Budget Day if prices drop -1.47% to -3.02% in three days that follow Budget Day

In the remaining 23 years with larger or weaker three-day drops, the record over the next three weeks was eight up and 15 down.

Other trends to watch

Putting the issue of Budget Day aside, there are a number of other trends that once helped investors to improve significantly the odds of making a profitable November investment. We don't know the degree to which Budget Day will affect these trends so use them with caution.

One formerly useful trend correlates November price shifts with the direction of prices in the last quarter of October. Since 1956, there have been 14 years when October fourth-quarter prices rose. November prices rose in 13 of those years (93%). Prices increased at a superb average rate of +3.18% per year, equal to 105 points on a 3300 FT-SE 100. The single exception was back in 1965 when Wilson warned the country of yet another economic crisis and imposed an import tax, on October 26th, and a 6% income tax increase, on November 11th. Even in that year, November prices fell by just -1.09%.

Rose (13)

Fell (1)

November trend after price rise in October's fourth quarter (since 1956)

Past 12 months

Another trend which, historically, has done a good job of anticipating the direction of November's price shifts is the direction of prices in the preceding 12 months. There have been 14 years in which share prices rose in the previous 12 months within a range of +20.00% to +36.86%. November prices rose in 12 of those years. The average November increase during these 14 years was +1.60%.

Rose (12)

Fell (2)

November trend after price rise in preceding 12 months of +20.00% to +36.86%

There have been 12 years in which prices shifted slightly in the last six months, within a range of -3.91% to +1.53%. November share prices rose in 11 of those years. The average November increase during these 12 years was +2.60%.

Rose (11)

Fell (1)

November trend after price shift in preceding six months of -3.91%
to +1.53%

The direction of prices over the past two months has flagged
some big November falls in the past. There have been nine years
in which share prices rose in the preceding two months by
+4.93% to +6.96%. November prices fell each time. The
average November decrease during these nine years was
-1.83%.

Rose (0)

Fell (9)

November trend after price rise in preceding two months of
+4.93% to +6.96%

First Quarter of November – November 1st to November 8th

The first quarter is just slightly profitable over the long-run.
Between 1935 and 1993, the record is 30 up (51%), 29 down
and an average profit of +0.09% per year (*see Table 12.2*). An
analysis of daily price trends during this quarter of the month
finds that the middle of the quarter is most profitable (*see Figure
12.2*).

Budget Day
influence

We don't yet know the effect of Budget Day on first-quarter
prices. Prior to the Budget Day switch, it was possible to
increase the odds of making a profit on the down-side in some
years by watching the direction of prices in the third *and* fourth
quarters of October. We first reported this relationship in the
1994 Investor's Diary. Here is a revised update. Since 1935,
there have been 12 years in which prices fell in October's third
and fourth quarter, with a fourth-quarter fall of at least -0.31%.
In 10 of those years, prices continued to fall in the first quarter

Table 12.2   **PERCENTAGE PRICE CHANGE NOVEMBER: 1935–1993**

	November 1–8	November 9–15	November 16–23	November 24–30
Average annual price change				
1935–39	0.70%	0.22%	-2.02%	0.27%
1940–49	0.70%	0.83%	0.74%	-0.05%
1950–59	-0.10%	0.16%	-0.43%	-0.20%
1960–69	-0.53%	2.10%	-1.44%	-0.07%
1970–79	-0.68%	-1.00%	-1.02%	-0.23%
1980–89	0.90%	1.40%	0.49%	-0.15%
1990–93	-0.34%	-0.55%	1.36%	1.30%
Average quarterly price change	0.09%	0.57%	-0.36%	-0.01%
Number of years in which prices:				
rose	30	36	27	30
fell	29	20	32	27
remained unchanged	–	3	–	2

Table 12.2: The first-quarter investor lost money in the 1950s–'70s, but things improved in the 1980s. The second quarter has been profitable in most decades. In contrast, the fourth quarter of November has been a steady money-loser.

---

of November. The average price drop was -1.67% in those 12 years, equal to 55 points on a 3300 FT-SE 100.

Rose (2)   [ ]

Fell (10)   [   ]

First-quarter trend after price drop in preceding two quarters with October's fourth quarter dropping at least -0.31%

Another trend worth watching is the direction of prices in the month of October. There have been nine occasions since 1935 when October prices fell -1.96% to -5.97%. Prices continued to

Figure 12.2   **PERCENTAGE OF TIME PRICES RISE EACH TRADING DAY IN NOVEMBER'S FIRST QUARTER**

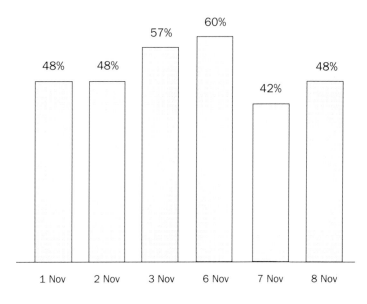

Figure 12.2: The best two days of the quarter are Friday, November 3, and Monday, November 6.

fall in the first quarter of November on all nine occasions. The average first-quarter price decline was -2.05%.

Rose (0)

Fell (9)

First-quarter trend after price drop in October by -1.96% to -5.97%

SECOND QUARTER OF NOVEMBER – NOVEMBER 9TH TO NOVEMBER 15TH

Second-quarter prices rose 61% of the time between 1935 and 1993, the best performance of the entire month. They rose at an average annual rate of +0.57%.

The second-quarter investor made money in every complete decade on record except for the 1970s. It was November's Number One-ranked quarter in the 1940s, '50s, '60s, and '80s. Analysis of price shifts on a day-by-day basis shows generally good trading conditions. The weakest day of the quarter is its first trading day, November 9th. But the odds of a profit soon improve (*see Figure 12.3*).

Figure 12.3

PERCENTAGE OF TIME PRICES RISE EACH TRADING DAY IN NOVEMBER'S SECOND QUARTER

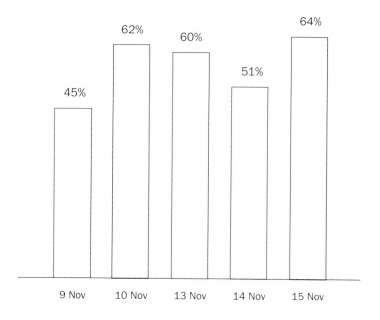

Figure 12.3: It is the best quarter of the month. There is a good chance of rising prices on most days in the quarter.

Possible Budget
Day effect

Here again, we don't know the effect of Budget Day on this quarter's prices. We previously reported that the price trends in the fourth quarter of October and the first quarter of November do a good job of forecasting a price rise in this quarter. Here's an update based on historical records collected before the Budget Day switch.

If prices rise in October's final quarter by +0.59% or more and either rise in November's first quarter, or fall by no more than -2.55%, they are very likely to rise in the second quarter. Since 1935, there have been 23 years in which prices shifted within the appropriate range in both periods. The price trend continued to rise through November's second quarter in 21 of those years (91%). The average price rise was +1.50%.

Rose (21)

Fell (2)

Second-quarter trend after price rise in October's fourth quarter of +0.59% or more and a rise in November's first quarter or a drop of no more than -2.55%

THIRD QUARTER OF NOVEMBER – NOVEMBER 16TH TO NOVEMBER 23RD

Historically, the third quarter is the month's worst performer, averaging an annual loss of -0.36%. Prices rose 27 times (46%) and fell 32 times.

The third-quarter investor lost money in the 1950s, '60s, and '70s. In the Bull Market 1980s, the quarter's performance improved with an average profit of +0.49%. But a look under the surface shows that nothing had really changed with a record of three up and seven down (see Table 12.3).

Worst day of
the month

The daily price trend is strongest during the first two days of the quarter, a continuation of good second-quarter trading conditions. Unfortunately, the odds of encountering a profitable trading day then slip dramatically. The November 22nd record (prices up just 31% of the time) is the worst trading day of the entire month (see Figure 12.4).

Table 12.4

PERCENTAGE PRICE CHANGE DURING NOVEMBER SINCE 1980

	November 1–8	November 9–15	November 16–23	November 24–30
1980	-2.03%	4.20%	3.89%	-4.21%
1981	5.55%	4.99%	-0.27%	3.86%
1982	2.82%	2.66%	-2.83%	-2.87%
1983	2.42%	1.00%	-0.40%	3.00%
1984	0.56%	2.08%	-0.17%	0.80%
1985	1.25%	0.33%	4.54%	0.66%
1986	2.47%	-1.82%	-1.47%	1.41%
1987	-6.39%	3.38%	-0.58%	-4.47%
1988	-0.71%	-2.02%	2.50%	-2.63%
1989	3.07%	-0.83%	-0.30%	2.94%
1990	-1.13%	1.57%	7.04%	-1.72%
1991	0.67%	-5.50%	-1.43%	0.00%
1992	2.12%	0.81%	0.63%	3.03%
1993	-3.03%	0.91%	-0.78%	3.89%
Average quarterly price change				
1980–89	0.90%	1.40%	0.49%	-0.15%
1980–93	0.55%	0.84%	0.74%	0.26%
Number of years in which prices:				
rose	9	10	5	8
fell	5	4	9	5
remained unchanged	–	–	–	1

Table 12.4: Sometimes you have to look beneath the surface to see the real story. The strong second-quarter trend continued into the 1990s with prices up in three out of four years. The average annual loss of -0.55% during this period was due to just one poor year, 1991. In contrast, the recent third-quarter average is better than its long-term trend due to three good years. Prices rose in just two of the other 11 years.

Figure 12.4 **PERCENTAGE OF TIME PRICES RISE EACH TRADING DAY IN NOVEMBER'S THIRD QUARTER**

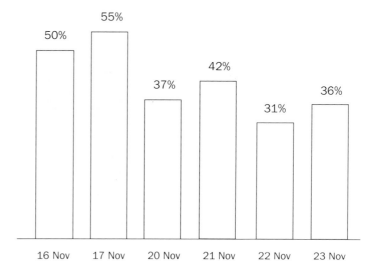

Figure 12.4: Second-quarter strength continues for the first two days of this quarter. The trend then significantly weakens, especially on November 22, the month's worst day.

Assuming a late November Budget Day, we hypothesise that it will exert a large influence on this part of November in the future. Prior to Budget Day being shifted to this part of the year, there was a good short-term down-side signal operating in this quarter. Out of 11 years when prices dropped in November's first half by -2.79% or worse, they continued to decline in the third quarter nine times (82%). The average annual decrease was -2.56%. We shall watch with interest to see if this signal remains viable.

Rose (2)

Fell (9)

Third-quarter trend after price drop of -2.79% or more in November's first half

FOURTH QUARTER OF NOVEMBER – NOVEMBER 24TH TO NOVEMBER 30TH

The fourth quarter of November used to be a poor time to be holding shares. Prices declined at an average annual rate of -0.01%. Between 1935 – 1993, the record was 30 up (51%), 27 down and two no change.

The fourth-quarter investor lost money in every complete decade for which we have records, from the 1940s to the 1980s. Judging from the daily price records, most of the damage occurs in the last two trading days of the month when prices rise just 41% of the time (*see Figure 12.5*).

Watch for
Budget Day

Budget Day will probably change things. Keep on the look out for the actual date that the budget will be presented. If Budget Day does land in this quarter, be warned: prices fall 71% of the time in the five days before Budget Day.

Figure 12.5

PERCENTAGE OF TIME PRICES RISE EACH TRADING DAY IN NOVEMBER'S FOURTH QUARTER

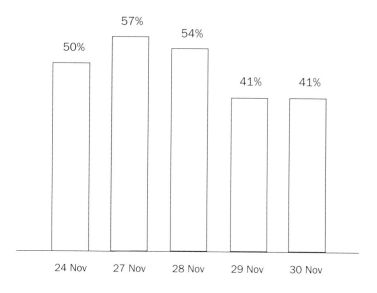

Figure 12.5: Historically, the final two days of November have been money-losers.

Here is one historical correlation that has helped investors to make money during this quarter in the past. It involves the direction of prices in the first three quarters of November. There have been eight occasions on record where prices rose in the first three quarters of November. Fourth-quarter prices continued to rise in seven of them (88%). The average yearly increase was +0.91%.

Rose (7)

Fell (1)

Fourth-quarter trend after prices rose in the first three quarters of November

Since 1952, there have been 12 years when third-quarter prices shifted very slightly, from -0.40% to +0.57%. Fourth-quarter prices rose in 10 of those years.

Rose (10)

Fell (2)

Fourth-quarter trend after third-quarter prices shifted by -0.40% to +0.57% (since 1952)

We will keep a careful watch on these trends to ensure they are still operative in the new November investing environment.

Chapter Thirteen – December 1995

The closest thing to a Christmas present the stock market offers

GED

December is a consistent money-maker. Since 1919, it has delivered an average price rise of +1.09% per year. Five of the 10 most profitable days in the entire year are in this great month. Better still, the month to follow is the year's best month making December the beginning of the best two-month period of the year. If you are thinking of buying shares, this is the month in which to do it.

December is a good month

Investors usually make money in December. Between 1919 and 1993, December prices rose 57% of the time. The average price rise was +1.09%, equal to 36 points on an FT-SE 100 in the area of 3300.[1] The constant December investor made an average annual profit in every decade on record, with the exception of the 1930s (*see Table 13.1*). A £1,000 December investment in 1919 would have grown to £2,131 by 1993.

---

[1] Reminder: All monthly calculations are based on the FT-Non-Financial Index, formerly the FT-'500'; unless otherwise stated, they are based on data from 1919–1993. All daily, quarterly, and bi-monthly calculations are based on the Ordinary Share Index, also known as the FT-30; unless otherwise stated, they are based on data from 1935-1993.

Table 13.1   **DECEMBER PRICE RISES AND DECLINES: 1919–1993**

	Average December price change	Up	Down/ no change
1920–29	0.57%	7	3
1930–39	-0.85%	5	5
1940–49	0.66%	4	6
1950–59	1.60%	7	3
1960–69	0.84%	5	5
1970–79	2.13%	5	5
1980–89	1.83%	6	4
1990–93	3.42%	4	–
Average December price change	1.09%	43	32

Table 13.1: The only loss-making decade was back in the 1930s. Since then, December has been consistently profitable.

Over the 75 years for which we have data, December is fourth-best in terms of monthly profitability, surpassed only by January, April and August.

... and getting better

The December record is getting better. Table 13.2 shows its performance over three successive 25 year periods. The size of the average annual profit and the likelihood of a price rise have steadily improved. The improvement continues right up to the present. In the 1980s, prices rose in six of the decade's 10 years, with an average monthly price rise of +1.83%. Although the jury is still out for the rest of the 1990s, the record to 1993 is four up and no declines.

The month often starts off slowly with losses at the beginning of the month. But things soon start to sizzle. The third and fourth quarters are usually profitable and are ranked, respectively, in third and first place for the entire year (see Figure 13.1). Investors should also recall that Number One-ranked January is just around the corner. The December to January period is the most profitable two-month stretch of the entire year.

The one fly in the ointment is the recent switch to a late-Autumn Unified Budget. We don't know for certain how the budget will affect December prices. Available evidence suggests there is nothing to fear:

Table 13.2

DECEMBER HAS BEEN IMPROVING

	Average annual price change	Up	Rank
1919–1943	-0.17%	13	7
1944–1968	1.11%	14	5
1969–1993	2.32%	16	3

Table 13.2: December's profitability has been steadily improving. In three successive 25-year periods, the month's average annual profit has risen as have the number of price rises and its ranking on monthly profitability.

▶ The period around Budget Day is usually good for investors.

▶ If a budget-related problem does occur, its main effect is often felt close to Budget Day, with the worst 'hits' occurring in the quarter or two adjacent to the budget's presentation.

▶ The strong performance of December's second half is probably influenced by end-of-year money flows and expectations about the year ahead, a pattern we expect to continue.

Our working hypothesis is that even in the aftermath of a poorly received budget, the second half of December should be distant enough to continue to enjoy favourable trading conditions. All of this is theory, of course. We will watch the situation carefully.

12-month trend

Although the overall December 'story' is a good one, there are several historical price trends that help investors to improve significantly the odds of making a profitable December investment. Here is one of the best. There have been 20 years in which share prices rose in the previous 12 months by at least +8.74% and in the previous two months by +0.96% to +7.94%. December prices rose in 19 of those years. The average profit was +2.37%. The single losing month was December 1941 when prices fell in the aftermath of Japan's December 7th sneak attacks and Britain's Declaration of War on December 8th.

Figure 13.1

PROFITABILITY OF DECEMBER'S FOUR QUARTERS

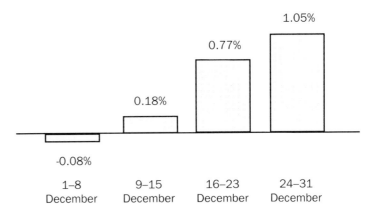

Figure 13.1: The month often starts off poorly for investors. But profits soon begin to appear in most years. The third and fourth quarters are among the most profitable segments of the year.

Rose (19)

Fell (1)

December's record after previous 12 month price rise of at least +8.74% and previous two-month rise of +0.96% to +7.94%

September to November

The price trend in the three months that precede December often provides good clues for the December investor. There have been 14 years when prices shifted between -1.74% to +5.96% in the preceding three months and rose by +0.61% to +5.58% in November. December share prices rose in every one of those years.

Rose (14)

Fell (0)

December's record after previous three-month shift of -1.74% to +5.96% and a November rise of +0.61% to +5.58%

If we eliminate duplication within these trends, there are 27 years that are flagged by at least one of them. The December record is 26 up and one down. In years untouched by either one of these two up-trend signals, December's record has been simply terrible – 19 up and 27 down, and two no change.

Watch for danger signals

Investors can improve the odds of identifying a declining December by watching the price trend during the preceding two months. In years untouched by one of the two up-trend forecasts, an October/November price rise within a range of +0.95% to +14.51% is an important red flag danger signal. Out of 21 months with price rises within this range, December prices fell 17 times.

Rose (4)

Fell (17)

December's record after an October/November price rise of +0.95% to +14.51% (in years untouched by either up-trend forecast)

FIRST QUARTER OF DECEMBER – DECEMBER 1ST TO DECEMBER 8TH

December may be a good month in which to invest – but not its first quarter. A decade-by-decade analysis reveals that the first quarter of the month is its least profitable segment. Prices rose in just 44% of all first quarters on record and produced an average loss of -0.08% per year (*see Table 13.3*).

To capitalise on a price drop – move quickly

The 1980s was especially weak with a record of four up, six down and an average annual loss of -0.59%. If you are thinking about betting on a price drop, one word of caution. When market conditions suggest a drop is especially likely, be prepared to move fast. Even if the second quarter continues to be weak, a trend that has been apparent in recent years, the year-end rally is likely to begin soon.

Analysis of daily price trends reveals significant weaknesses on December 4th. Prices rise just 36% of the time. This pattern continues right up to the present. Since 1984, the December 4th record is one up and seven down (*see Figure 13.2*).

Table 13.3 **PERCENTAGE PRICE CHANGE: DECEMBER 1935–1993**

	December 1–8	December 9–15	December 16–23	December 24–31
Average annual price change				
1935–39	-0.63%	0.12%	0.40%	0.73%
1940–49	0.05%	0.29%	0.54%	0.67%
1950–59	0.18%	1.20%	0.36%	1.11%
1960–69	-0.63%	0.69%	-0.06%	0.88%
1970–79	0.54%	-1.24%	1.93%	1.49%
1980–89	-0.59%	-0.08%	1.33%	1.01%
1990–93	0.66%	0.38%	0.67%	1.69%
Average quarterly price change	-0.08%	0.18%	0.77%	1.05%
Number of years in which prices:				
rose	26	34	42	48
fell	33	23	15	10
remained unchanged	–	2	2	1

Table 13.3: The first quarter is December's weak link. Prices rise less than half the time. Fortunately, the third and fourth quarters make up for the poor start. Their strong performance is a long-term phenomenon. On a decade-by-decade basis, they are virtually always the best two quarters of the month.

November's second half

With the switch to a late-year Budget Day, we caution investors that historic trend forecasts may be less reliable than usual. Nevertheless, here is one trend that formerly worked well. Since 1942, there were 10 years with a small price shift in November's second half, no more than -0.48% on the down-side and no more than +0.58% on the up-side. First-quarter prices fell in nine of those years at an average of -1.19% per year. The single exception occurred in 1944.

Rose (1) ☐

Fell (9) ☐

First-quarter record after a price shift of -0.48% to +0.58% in November's second half (since 1942)

Figure 13.2 **PERCENTAGE OF TIME PRICES RISE EACH TRADING DAY IN DECEMBER'S FIRST QUARTER**

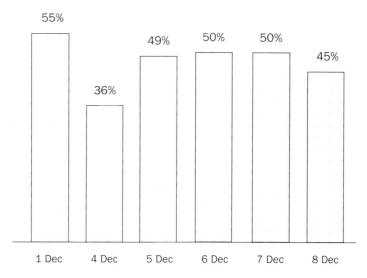

Figure 13.2: Prices often fall on December 4. Since 1984, the record is one up and seven down.

SECOND QUARTER OF DECEMBER – DECEMBER 9TH TO DECEMBER 15TH

Our historical review of all second-quarter closing prices sends an exceedingly clear message. If you were thinking about buying shares in the near future, the time to do it is fast approaching.

Since 1935, second-quarter closing prices rose 58% of the time and produced an average annual profit of +0.18%.

But don't be too quick to jump into the market at the very beginning of this quarter. The long-term trend is changing, unfortunately for the worse. In the last 20 years, from 1974 to 1993, the second-quarter record has been quite poor – eight up and 12 down. Things have not changed much since 1987. The recent record is two up and four down (*see Table 13.4*).

Table 13.4   **PERCENTAGE PRICE CHANGE DURING DECEMBER SINCE 1980**

	December 1–8	December 9–15	December 16–23	December 24–31
1980	-5.06%	-1.02%	0.50%	1.67%
1981	-2.99%	-1.57%	0.82%	2.45%
1982	-2.08%	0.43%	0.31%	1.41%
1983	1.89%	-0.97%	2.95%	0.09%
1984	0.62%	1.34%	-1.19%	3.03%
1985	-2.21%	-1.05%	0.69%	1.61%
1986	-1.29%	0.38%	1.12%	-0.86%
1987	3.52%	2.87%	6.56%	-3.25%
1988	-1.43%	-0.68%	0.62%	1.33%
1989	3.12%	-0.55%	0.89%	2.59%
1990	2.44%	-1.31%	-0.75%	-0.87%
1991	-2.03%	3.39%	-4.43%	6.19%
1992	-0.22%	-1.14%	4.62%	1.04%
1993	2.45%	0.59%	3.26%	0.40%
Average quarterly price change				
1980–89	-0.59%	-0.08%	1.33%	1.01%
1980–93	-0.23%	0.05%	1.14%	1.20%
Number of years in which prices:				
rose	6	6	11	11
fell	8	8	3	3

Table 13.4: The recent trend for each quarter mirrors the patterns of the past. First- and second-quarter prices are relatively weak, third- and fourth-quarter prices, relatively strong.

Analysis of daily price trends reveals that the beginning of the quarter is relatively weak. Be especially watchful on December 11th. Since 1984, prices rose once and fell seven times (*see Figure 13.3*).

Caution   The implication for investors? Be cautious. But don't back away from shares too far. Keep in mind that the trend for the following seven quarters is quite good. A strategy that worked well recently was to buy on second-quarter weakness.

Here is one trend that has done a good job of forecasting

Figure 13.3

PERCENTAGE OF TIME PRICES RISE EACH TRADING DAY IN DECEMBER'S SECOND QUARTER

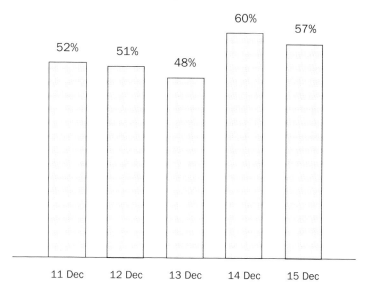

Figure 13.3: December 11 rises 52% of the time. Unfortunately, since 1984, its record has been poor – one up and seven down.

rising second-quarter prices. If shares shift within a narrow range of -0.91% to +2.49% in November's second half, and -0.71% to +1.22% in December's first quarter, they will probably rise in the second quarter. There have been 15 years with price shifts within these ranges. Second-quarter prices rose in 14 of them. The average increase was +1.19% .

Rose (14)

Fell (1)

Second-quarter record after a price shift of -0.91% to +2.49% in November's second half and -0.71% to +1.22% in December's first quarter

Keep in mind that Budget Day may have affected this trend. We shall watch the situation carefully.

THIRD QUARTER OF DECEMBER – DECEMBER 16TH TO DECEMBER 23RD

December's third quarter has been a nice little money-earner during the past 59 years. Even more important, it marks the beginning of a profitable stretch that runs through to early February. While you would not have profited in every single quarter nor in every single year, the record shows that between 1935 to 1993, the average share price rose sharply during this seven-quarter stretch.

A hypothetical start-up investment of £1,000 in 1974, placed in shares during these seven quarters, and in cash for the rest of the year, would have grown to £6,124 by 1993. If you consider that the investment was at risk for about 700 trading days in total (roughly three years of normal trading) the size of this profit is easier to grasp.

The third quarter is usually profitable

Focusing on December's third quarter reveals that prices have risen in 71% of all years on record. The only segment of the year which rose more often was December's fourth quarter which rose 81% of the time. Third-quarter share prices have increased by an average annual rate of +0.77%.

The worst-ever decade for the third quarter was in the 1960s when investors lost at an average rate of -0.06% per year. But even then, the record was six up and four down. Many of the price moves of that decade were small. As a result, the biggest decline of the decade, a relatively small -3.84% in 1967 had a much larger effect on the decade's average than similar sized declines usually have.

The 1980s continued the good profits trend with a record of nine up and one down, and an average annual profit of +1.33%.

We shall have to wait and see whether the pattern continues through the 1990s. The record since 1990 is two up and two down and an average annual profit of 0.67%.

December 22nd

Analysis of share price trends on a day-by-day basis reveals that prices rise 74% of the time on December 22nd, the year's third-best day. December 23 and 24 are also in the year's Top 10 (*see Figure 13.4 and Table 13.5*). Unfortunately, both of these days fall on a weekend in 1995. But don't fret. When stock markets are closed on December 23rd and/or 24th, the odds of making a profit remain high on the final pre-Christmas trading day (either the 22nd or 23rd). There have been 20 years since

Figure 13.4

PERCENTAGE OF TIME PRICES RISE EACH TRADING DAY IN DECEMBER'S THIRD QUARTER

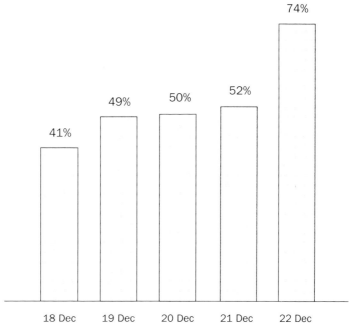

Figure 13.4: The week before Christmas has a secret weapon, December 22, where prices rise 74% of the time. It is the year's third-best performance.

1935 with a final pre-Christmas trading day not being December 24th. Prices fell on just one of those days (5%).

We notice that the third quarter has been quite volatile in the past three years. The drop of -4.43% in 1991, the biggest ever, was followed by increases of +4.62% in 1992 and +3.26% in 1993. We shall watch these new developments with great interest.

There are a number of ways to improve the odds of making a third-quarter profit. One trick is to watch the price trend in the first two quarters of the month. If prices rise in both periods, or if they fall in both periods, the chance of a third-quarter profit improves significantly. We first mentioned this phenomenon in the *1994 Investor's Diary*. Here is an improved update.

Watch the first half

Since 1943, there have been 13 occasions when the price of an average share rose in each of the first two quarters of the

195

Table 13.5   **THE BEST DAYS OF THE YEAR**

	Percent of time prices rise
December 24	80%
December 27	79%
April 27	74%
December 22	74%
December 29	71%
August 3	71%
December 23	70%
April 15	69%
June 6	69%
April 3	68%

Table 13.5: It's simply unbelievable. Five of the year's 10 best days arrive in December. All occur after December 21.

month. The third-quarter record in those 13 years was 11 increases (85%), two losing quarters and an average annual third-quarter profit of +1.25%. This signal last flashed in 1993 and prices rose +3.26% in the third quarter.

Rose (11)

Fell (2)

Third-quarter record after a price rise in the first and second quarter of December (since 1943)

There were an additional 11 years when the price of the average share fell in both preceding quarters. Prices rose in eight of those years, remained unchanged in two and fell just once.

Rose (8)

Fell (1)

No change (2)

Third-quarter record after a price drop in the first and second quarters of December

The second-quarter trend, by itself, also does a fine job of forecasting third-quarter increases in share price. There have been 24 years with a very small second-quarter price shift in the range of -1.14% to +0.61%. Third-quarter prices rose in 23 of those years. The single exception was back in 1957.

Rose (23)

Fell (1)

Third-quarter record after a price shift in the second quarter of -1.14% to +0.61%

FOURTH QUARTER OF DECEMBER – DECEMBER 24TH TO DECEMBER 31ST

Investors frequently profit during the fourth quarter of December. It is the very best quarter of the entire year. Three of the 10 best days of the entire year are in this segment of December.

Between 1936–1993, prices rose, unbelievably, 81% of the time. The average annual gain was +1.05%. Both figures are the best of all 48 quarters of the year.

The year's best quarter

The fourth segment of the month has produced an average annual profit in every decade on record. The 'worst' decade was the 1940s when the average annual profit was just +0.67%, equivalent to 22 points on an FT-SE 100 in the area of 3300.

The recent trend has been as strong as ever. The record for the Bull Market 1980s was eight up, two down, and an average annual profit of +1.01%. Since 1990, the fourth quarter has risen in three of the past four years at an average of +1.69% per year.

In the period covering the final two trading days before Christmas and the three (or so) trading days between Christmas and New Year's Day, share prices fell just eight times in the 59 years between 1935 and 1993 (14%). It is the closest thing to a guaranteed profit that the stock market will ever offer.

Analysis of share price trends on a daily basis shows above-average strength throughout this quarter (*see Figure 13.5*). The third quarter does a fine job of helping investors to identify a

Figure 13.5

PERCENTAGE OF TIME PRICES RISE EACH TRADING DAY IN DECEMBER'S FOURTH QUARTER

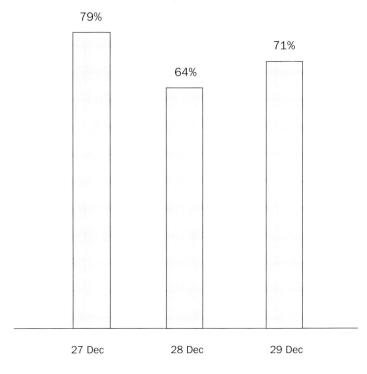

Figure 13.5: The fourth quarter may be holiday-shortened, but prices tend to rise on the few days that trading does occur. December 27 is the year's second-best day. December 29 is the year's fifth-best day.

profitable fourth quarter. There have been 29 third quarters with small price shifts within a range of -0.19% to +0.89%. Fourth-quarter prices fell in just one of those years, a -0.09% fall (equal to three points on a 3300 FT-SE 100) back in 1950. The average annual increase was +1.33%.

Rose (28)

Fell (1)

Fourth-quarter record after a price shift in the third quarter of -0.19% to +0.89%